Addiction's Many Faces

Tackling drug dependency amongst young people: causes, effects and prevention

Felicitas Vogt

Hawthorn Press

Published by Hawthorn Press, Hawthorn House, 1 Lansdown Lane, Stroud, Gloucestershire, GL5 1BJ, UK Tel: (01453) 757040 Fax: (01453) 751138
www.hawthornpress.com

Cover images by Michael Chase, The Mask Studio, Stourbridge
Typesetting and cover design by Hawthorn Press, Stroud, Gloucestershire
Printed in the UK by The Cromwell Press, Trowbridge, Wiltshire

First published in Germany in 2000 by aethera im Verlag Freies Geistesleben & Urachhaus, under the title *Sucht hat viele Gesichter*.

This edition © Hawthorn Press 2002
Translated by Matthew Barton

British Library Cataloguing in Publication Data applied for

ISBN 1 903458 17 X

About this book

From her many years' experience as teacher and addiction counsellor, Felicitas Vogt describes the inner and outer influences which can lead to addiction. These are nowadays more prevalent than ever before: children and young people today are confronted by situations which demand enormous emotional endurance of them.

Further themes are the consequences and risks of drug-taking, various drugs and their effects, the underlying reasons leading to addiction, stages and methods of withdrawal, and preventive measures. Much space is also devoted to original transcripts of conversations with young people, which are more expressive and insightful than any number of clever theories.

About the author

Felicitas Vogt was born in Cologne in 1952, and studied theology and sport. For twelve years she was a class-teacher at the Würzburg Waldorf school. From her student days she helped people who got caught up in sects, or who were hooked on drugs. In 1988 she began giving lectures and seminars on the themes of addiction, prevention and life questions, and from 1994 onwards has worked for the medical and pedagogical section at the Goetheanum in Dornach.[1] Since 1996 she has been secretary of the association for anthroposophical health-care in Bad Liebenzell.

1   The international headquarters of the Anthroposophical Society, based on the work of Rudolf Steiner

Contents

Preface

Some years ago a World Health Organisation forecast hit the news: if drug and medicine abuses increase as fast as in the previous twenty years, it said, then by 2010 every second person would be addicted to drugs. What do such figures tell us? What message are they giving? At present, literature on drugs is marked by two opposite tendencies: normalisation of drug consumption and the battle against it.

Ought we not to accept as normal something that every adolescent has to face, and which will soon confront every child too? Or should we step up our efforts to prevent, monitor, control, punish and treat this evil, in order to get a grip on it? What is usually disregarded however, is the fact that addiction, dependency and drug use have never before in human history been such a problem in adolescence and, increasingly, in childhood. They are typical signs of our times, and will become still more prevalent as we enter the twenty-first century.

When I first met Felicitas Vogt many years ago, at a youth conference organised by young people themselves, our discussion soon turned to the mission of the drugs theme in the lives of young people. Why has it been so much a part of the twentieth century? What can and must we all learn from it – as contemporaries, fellow travellers?

Felicitas Vogt places this question at the centre of her book. At the same time it seems as if the many young people with whom she has worked have co-written it, helping to find a form for it which young people themselves can relate to. But I also hope that parents and educators not directly affected will turn to it to find out why the theme of drugs and addiction might concern them, even if they have neglected it before. May this book succeed in stimulating people apparently unaffected by drug-taking and addictive behaviour, to acknowledge their social responsibility and involvement.

Michaela Glöckler
The medical section at the Goetheanum
Midsummer 2000

Drug use – whether alcohol, hard or soft drugs – is widespread. I only have to walk up our local high street at lunch time for a coffee(!) with a friend to meet several people who are drug-users and also to be offered drugs myself. So young people – naturally keen to find out about the world – need to be well-informed about the causes and effects of drug abuse. They can then decide for themselves what is healthy and also cope more effectively with 'drug-pushing'. And it can be difficult to stand up for yourself, even though you are well-informed and have strong family support. For example, a local teenage girl attempted suicide after being bullied by a powerful peer group trying to force her to take drugs.

Currently in Britain, 49% of 16-29 year olds have tried an illegal drug, and a third of 15-16 year olds are using or dabbling in drugs regularly.[1] One survey found that on average, their drug-using clients first began using drugs at 16, but it was only at 22 when this was perceived as a problem, and 26 when they sought help. This shows the crucial importance of early discussion and diagnosis with young people at risk by parents, teachers and friends.

Addiction's Many Faces offers a practical and sensible approach to helping families understand drug issues, so parents can feel secure and confident in their ability to discuss these important questions openly with their children. As parents, we face a difficult and sometimes confusing world where it can be easy to withdraw from or ignore the challenge of drugs. However, this useful guide will help make sense of the question of addiction, so as to remove fears with real insight and informed action.

Martin Large
Author of *Who's Bringing Them Up?*

1 Figures from British Crime Survey 1998, University of Manchester for Drugs Prevention Advisory Service 1999, and Addaction's Annual Report 2000

Foreword

Are you sure you're not addicted or dependent? In any way? Most of us are, though some of our addictions may be subtle and concealed. As this book points out, substance addiction is just one very obvious form of addiction. You too, therefore, are likely to have inner connections with the themes in these pages! You don't think so? But perhaps you reach a little compulsively for your coffee in the morning? Or maybe you meant to read that book you bought last month, but find yourself regularly slumped in front of the telly instead? Do you find it hard to avoid criticising people – perhaps the negative words just spill out unawares? Mull over your findings. I expect you'll agree that changing some of our habits is hard work.

As the author points out, addiction and freedom are two sides of the same coin. The book's unique angle relates to addiction's potential mission in our time, showing how those who hold their addictions at bay and overcome them can be better equipped – stronger – to fulfil their purpose in life. Addiction is therefore not just negative, but a hard school in which we can learn self-fulfilment through conquering our dependencies.

At the root of much addiction is pain. Addictive substance (mis)use blocks out the heartache that would arise if we really faced our troubles. In my therapeutic work in a drug rehab with women and children, the recovering mums can feel overwhelmed by the consequences of their former lifestyles: children subject to Child Protection Orders and some ending up in foster homes; babies born withdrawing from the opiates they got addicted to in the womb; mother and child with blood-borne infections such as Hepatitis C; and prostitution as a life choice to fund addiction and support the family financially. What a lot of baggage addiction creates.

We know the horror stories. But what I particularly like about this book is that the author continually stresses the importance of searching for non-judgemental ways of meeting young people's needs to help them avoid or overcome addiction. In my former job as a drug prevention worker in a deprived area of Glasgow, I noticed a clear divide between groups of adults who were involved in action-on-drugs initiatives. Some were 'at war' with drugs while others were 'soft' or liberal about young drug users. This book takes neither approach but instead invites us to really face the complex issues around drugs and addiction. It encourages us to fight dependency but also, above all, to understand the pain young people often endure nowadays.

In this book, too, young people themselves speak out. If you want to understand the experiences they are seeking from drugs, if you want indications on how to relate to young drug (ab)users, if you want ideas about dealing with drug use in school environments – then read these stories.

At the same time we should remember the predicament of parents, often standing helplessly on the sidelines as their children experiment with drugs. What is the best way for parents to respond? This book has both sympathy and suggestions for adults seeking answers, including some straight talking about drug facts. Readers will find a useful section on different types of drugs and their effects in these pages.

Then there is prevention, which the author sees as inextricably linked to developing healthy 'forces' in childhood. She argues that if parents and educators work to strengthen the forces of childhood, the pay-off for children in later years could be in-built resistance to the paths of substance misuse and addiction. But are we ready to alter how we live with or educate children to strengthen these forces? And how do we begin to do this?

Finally, a short inspiring piece at the end of the book describes a form of intervention called anthroposophical drug therapy. This section should interest drug workers looking for fresh impulses for their work. Being a fan of addiction work based on Rudolf Steiner's ideas, I'm delighted to announce here that Britain's first anthroposophical residential addiction treatment centre is being planned in Stroud, Gloucestershire (see page 105).

I recommend this book to anyone studying addiction or those who pluck up courage to tackle their own dependency issues. It offers a careful, calm, hopeful approach through a potential mine-field of issues.

Frank O'Hare,
Dip. Addiction, Dip. Biographical Counselling,
ACOSCA, Glasgow

Introduction

I have learned one thing from 20 years of involvement with addiction and all its manifestations: addictive tendencies are as much a part of our time as opportunities for self-determination and freedom. Let me state it more boldly:

No opportunity for freedom without the danger of addiction!

Anyone who wishes to eliminate addiction and its dangers, would be depriving humanity of the chance to become more free through the battle against dependency.

But what does this mean for our children's generation, which must inevitably encounter addiction and drugs because they are a part of their world – much more so, in fact, than we adults often imagine? How can we help our children in this encounter and strengthen their powers of judgement?

Let us try to meet the phenomenon of addiction, and all that goes with it, in all the different realms where it manifests, with a fresh mind – open, searching, questioning, without ready-made answers.

If we can find out – from what people affected by this problem say, from the addiction phenomenon itself, from its actual circumstances and causes, from what people say who really have a sense of the way things are going nowadays – how far we ourselves are affected, then this encounter can lead us to our *own inner confrontation with addiction and drugs.*

Nothing can link us more vitally with our children and young people, with fellow human beings caught up in addiction, than our own inner involvement in this theme!

I would like to thank here the many people – parents and teachers as well as pupils – who in countless open and honest discussions entered with me on a process that was rarely comfortable or easy. This book is dedicated to them.

Felicitas Vogt
Easter 2000

Freedom in the deepest sense of the word means more
than saying what I think with no holds barred.
Freedom means that I also see the other,
that I put myself in his place
and, by sensitively grasping all this, that I am able
to extend my freedom
through empathy.
For what else is mutual understanding but
extending freedom and deepening truth?

Vaclav Havel

1

Drugs – just part of growing up?

Michael

Michael has come voluntarily for counselling. He's slouched on a chair opposite me and starts talking in an easy conversational tone: 'I heard you could help me – not sure exactly what with, but somehow I'm not coping too well.'

'Ah, you're not coping too well at the moment.'

'Well, what I mean is, at the moment I'd say I'm a bit weak-willed.'

'I see, you'd describe yourself as weak-willed.'

'Yes, that's what I said, yes. Not always, but I just don't always do what I would like to.'

'You're saying that you plan to do something but then you don't actually do it.'

'Yes, that's what I said; I don't quite manage things, and I thought you might be able to help me.'

'You thought I'd be able to help with this.'

'Yes. Why do you keep repeating what I say the whole time?'

'I want to be sure that I'm understanding you properly.'

'Yes, I'd like you to help me to be able to do what I intend to again.'

'You're asking me to help you to do what you intend? Are you serious about this?'

'Yes, I'm absolutely serious.'

Pause, a long pause.

'Michael, I have a feeling I know why you might be weak-willed at the moment.'

'Ok, yes, I've smoked a bit more dope than usual recently, that might have something to do with it.'

'Michael, you mean that being weak-willed might partly be connected with you smoking dope?'

'Yes, that's what I said. It's possible, don't you think?'

'Michael, let me repeat what you said: You suspect that smoking dope might have something to do with you being weak-willed.'

'Yes, that's what I suspect.'

'Michael, what do you suggest could be done about it?'

'OK, yes, I could stop, but I never know how to stop.'

'You don't know how to stop, but you know that if you did you'd be stronger-willed again.'

'Yes, and a friend of mine at school told me that you did it for him. He gave up. And now I'd like you to do the same for me.'

'Michael, I think there's a misunderstanding here. If you try to make me a kind of substitute drug, I have to tell you now that I can't help you.

What we can do, though, is to try to find out together how you can stop smoking dope. But only if you really want to. Not because I want you to, but only if you want it.'

The conversation continues like this for $1^{1}/2$ hours. Then it ends without any conclusion. He says he will get in touch again if he still feels he needs to.

After three months I get a phone call:

'Hi Mrs. Vogt, Michael here. I just wanted to tell you I did it, you probably know...'

'How did you manage it?'

'Well, that conversation of ours…'

'But I didn't even get as far as telling you how you could go about it…'

'Yeah, exactly… that's why.'

> 'The ego needs certain conditions for growth. It nourishes itself exclusively from its own impulses. What others do for it is not only not a help but merely weakens it. If the ego does not go half-way towards things out of its own impulse, the world repels it, constricts it and does not cease doing so until the ego gives up or dies.'[1]

Michael is on his way. He has understood that drugs-counselling does not mean that I, rather than the drug, should direct his life. He has understood that he has to discover the spark of self-determination in himself – and that he can't do this without exerting his will.

What I have learned from many counselling sessions with young drug-takers is that it is not I who can help, but only they who can find their way out of drugs. Struggling together to find the causes and reasons for their drug habit can waken their own inner activity. If young people can experience the free space of their own decision, the strength can grow to free themselves from the drug. This applies to young people from the age of 16 or 17. Younger teenagers naturally need other forms of help and also clear boundaries.

One aim of my conversations with young people is to create a basis for their own conscious decision. To do this one first has to offer them clear, objective information on the whole question of drugs and addiction. The next step is to characterise dependent and addictive behaviour. One has to open up the theme of the ego, of its freedom and responsibility. If both parties can openly acknowledge their own potential for addiction, the young person's previously largely self-focused assessment of his drug habit can broaden significantly. This basis gives him the necessary space of freedom to judge his addictive behaviour more objectively and autonomously – an essential precondition for a free decision.

> Great Spirit,
> protect me from
> judging another,
> before I have walked a mile
> in his moccasins.
>
> Unknown Apache warrior[2]

In contrast, all moral expectations that come towards a young person from outside must, at this age, be experienced as an attack on his own sphere of freedom, and therefore be rejected.

Here we adults, both parents and teachers, must learn to offer increasing space and freedom to our young people as their readiness for responsibility grows. Young people are often right to reproach us when they say that our fixed ideas of the best way to live prevent them from going their own, individual way.

Our wonderful world

Hurray, we're feeling really good!
We're only doing what we please.
So what if others lie in blood –
The world's ills aren't up to us.
There's war in the Congo – that's just tough!
People are dying – let them die!
All that counts is that we've enough
Food to stuff our faces in the usual way!

Hurray we're feeling really great!
Afghanistan? What's all the fuss?
Where is it anyway? Why get uptight?
Who cares, it's never bothered us!
As long as they leave us alone:
Just imagine if they all came over –
Those who do should bugger off home

Back to their own problems, leave us in clover!

Hurray, we're feeling really good!
Why should we bother with the poor?
Those wasters revelling in blood –
Charity starts at our own front door!

Hurray, we're feeling really good!
For we are wealthy in the West.
And if the Africans have got it hard –
So what, it's we who are the best.
We need their paper, coffee, wood
And pay them with our well-earned cash.
With huge and all-consuming greed
We buy the whole world to look flash.

Hurray, we're feeling fabulous!
We've got money, we've got food.
Dear old England is so nice,
We've got power, we've got it made!
We're not interested at all,
We're not interested, no way –
Why stop enjoying life to the full
Just 'cos people are dying far away?

If we're honest all of us know
That some of us tend to think like this.
And if we just stand by and do
Nothing the third world will get worse.
But if we'd stop talking now and act
And start to change things for the good,
We could transform the earth – and that's a fact;
And help the needy to a better world!!!

Poem by a class eleven pupil (age 17)

Young people today

Young people's protest against the modern world is something we experience everywhere. As outcry, such as in this poem, or as flight and avoidance through drug habits and anorexia; or alternatively, we see their resignation, expressed in apathy and conformism.

The drama of the adolescent unfolds in the confrontation of his[3] own burgeoning inner life with the external world. Unbounded openness to the outer world, to another person perhaps, alternates with wholesale rejection of it. Sympathy and antipathy are lived out in extreme and radical form – a spectrum which ranges from will-less dependency on a group in gangs and sects, through to uncompromising rejection of one's own body. Where a young person's inner world becomes the only core value, existential confrontations with the external world occur.

Today's adolescent is characterised by individualism. He is very wary of being pigeon-holed under *one single* concept, under one group or set of attachments. Fashion-dictated 'trademarks' and status symbols are more a kind of mask than a group characteristic.

Young people have always developed their identity through emphasis on their own, individual attributes. In particular young people distinguish themselves from the established, adult world by wearing strident, unusual clothing and shocking outfits.

Nowadays however, this way of setting themselves apart from the adult world has grown less and less available to them. Every provocative gesture is immediately seized on by society and marketed. This is what happened with the punk movement, whose style and clothing soon became all the rage and could soon be purchased in every trendy shop. The same is true of piercing and the techno scene. What was still shocking provocation a few years back, is swallowed up as fashionable style – worn even by an older generation.

So it becomes pretty hard for young people to clearly differentiate themselves from adults. But there are still commonly shared characteristics which distinguish today's adolescents:

The mask is part of this, behind which one's own inner life with its hidden longings is concealed more strongly than ever.

Inner attitudes to life, life-themes and goals are nowadays experienced as more intimate and kept more hidden than the former taboo issue of sexuality.

The longing for exhilaration and intoxication, for threshold experiences that break through a one-sided attachment to the material world and get away from the head-focused nature of our times, is also common among young people.

Bungee jumping, extreme forms of sport and endurance, adventure trips, even the real risk of death are an expression of this.

Moritz:

In another climbing accident I was briefly in danger of death; and I experienced my whole life unfurling before me like a film in coloured images. I've heard of this same experience from others. This made a strong impression on me, for I also saw my bad days. I think the experience changed me.[4]

Axel:

For me there are two types of adventure: bungee jumping-type ones, where you're simply out to get a kick; and mountain climbing adventures, which are to do with making a great effort.

When we've been walking the whole day and finally reach our destination in the evening, perhaps after various problems along the way, we feel really pleased. So pleased that it makes you feel kind of full inside. Other adventures, on the other hand, are maybe more spectacular, give you a 'high', but the effect doesn't last so long, or you get a 'downer' afterwards. I think there are many different ways and means. You just have to separate the grain from the chaff. When I look back on my school days, the really great experiences were going on camp, class trips and projects. Real challenges and exciting projects ought to have more of a place in school. In my work as youth leader I found out how valuable demanding trips are for children. After a climbing expedition, potholing or archaeology field trip the children are simply different in themselves: more assured and steady, but also more aware of their responsibility; for we place great value on consideration for others and taking responsibility.[5]

… for we place great value on consideration for others and taking responsibility…

Young people want to take responsibility, now as before, and form social ties. They want to have a deep experience of relationships, burst the bounds of their separateness and isolation and open themselves to others.

But they have rarely learned to overcome the hurdles which stand in their way. That is why it is so alluring for many of them to seek help from some substance, which joins them (the joint!) with others. The hashish joint gives a sense of being connected with others, of belonging together, of experiencing one's surroundings more intensely and vividly, of melting into them. The tempting fact that these experiences, which are fully justified in themselves, can seemingly be gained without any activity or effort of one's own, leads many young people into a hashish dependency from which they are almost unable to free themselves again.

That poses some urgent questions for us adults:

- Are we affected by the expressed and unexpressed longings of our adolescents in this world of materialism, unemployment, leisure activities without spiritual content, and social disintegration?
- Do we listen out for what comes towards us from young people? Are we concerned about the real conditions that they need in order to realise their wishes and needs?
- Do we perceive those questions which young people pose us in many unexpressed rather than expressed forms:
  - *Am I needed in this world? Do I have a task here?*
  - *How can I find my life's aims?*
  - *Are there people who hear my unexpressed questions?*
  - *Am I truly perceived?*
  - *What is my importance? Am I in any way unique?*
  - *What is freedom? What is love?*

Many young people secretly feel guilty for all sorts of things – also for many actions and reactions of adults. Somewhat along the lines of: 'I'm the problem;... without me you'd be better off;... you don't really want me;... I'm just a burden to you...', they often struggle with or are even obsessed by the idea of just 'getting rid' of themselves. So much hurt is expressed in this...

The longing to experience oneself as a creative, talented being, and as such to participate in fulfilling relationships and ways of living is the most vulnerable place in the adolescent soul today. In our society young people no longer live in a secure social context that assigns each individual a clear and certain place. They rarely experience adults around them who emanate calm and assurance, to whom they can look for direction.

In one counselling session a young person expressed this as

follows: 'You adults are incapable of really meeting each other – I find only masks; you're incapable of conflict – I see only self-justification; you're incapable of perceiving things – you don't see anything at all but just have pigeon-holes to put my behaviour in. You're so exhausted and burned-out that I don't want to bother you with my problems as well. You don't radiate any joy in life at all. I don't get any sense of the purpose of life from you.'

These are grave accusations, representative of the numerous unexpressed ones of all other young people who feel adults have left them in the lurch. They are justified reproaches, for who among us really finds the strength to get to grips with adolescents and their problems, and offer the necessary resistance against which they can push? This resistance would offer young people some direction and above all warmth, both of which they need more urgently than ever.

If they do not find this meeting and resistance with their 'own' adults, they seek it elsewhere – in extreme activities, threshold experiences; or instead they imitate us and avoid problems and conflicts, trying through substitute experiences to satisfy their deeply hidden longings in whatever way they can.

Benjamin

Benjamin has been forced to come to a drugs counselling session with me.

One can almost see his father's hand pushing him into the room, and then withdrawing. Benjamin is alone in the room with me.

Arrogant, indignant – he has no idea what he's supposed to be doing here.

Embarrassed silence. I offer him a friendly greeting.

Benjamin: 'OK, let's get on with it then. I've heard you know a lot about THC.'

'What would you like to know about THC?'

'Well, like, what does it do to the brain and that sort of thing. I've heard it can damage the brain, but I'm not convinced that's true.'

I describe the effect of tetrahydrocannabinol to Benjamin, and the fact that it paralyses and halts certain very specific processes; that smoking hash affects one's liver, will-activity, and the capacity to work towards goals in one's life etc...

None of this is new to Benjamin. He demonstrates this in radical fashion, unmistakeably: he keeps testing me, asks me clever questions.

After an hour of this 'examination' he ends the conversation, stands up and goes. I have a terrible feeling of failure.

That bore no relation to drugs counselling: it was a test which I failed with a young person.

Half an hour later the telephone rings. The boy's mother is phoning to ask how the session went. She sounds very expectant, hopeful that her boy's drugs problem is about to be solved. I have to disappoint her and tell her it did not go as expected. I ask her to let her son himself choose whether he would like to come and see me again or not.

He comes again a fortnight later. Continuation of the test situation. I interrupt the back and forth of questions and answers, and ask him what it is he really wants to know. He doesn't understand why he should be expelled from school because of his dope smoking habit, which now amounts to 2-3 joints a day. He can't understand it. When I ask him if he also deals he doesn't answer. I try to explain to him that teachers have a duty to protect both him and other pupils from the effect of the drug, that teachers have the right to expect to be able to teach in a drug-free environment. He can see that, but: none of this relates to him.

We agree on another meeting, together with his parents, with teachers he trusts, and with his therapist.

We get embroiled in repeated conversations in which Benjamin argues us under the table. He is clever, intelligent, quick, good at arguing. Our conversations keep taking their usual course – we have to watch out that he doesn't 'wipe the floor' with us.

At some point I grow angry and say: 'Benjamin, I'm not going to be part of this discussion any more. Stop this, we're just going round in circles. Either take your drugs or join a monastery!'

That is the turning point of our sessions together. Benjamin opens his eyes wide and says: 'Couldn't you have said that at our first meeting?'

I am surprised, pause, and for a moment am unsure whether he's referring to the drugs or the monastery. He says the monastery is a brilliant idea, for that's the nub of his problem. For the first time, stammering, doubtful, no longer argumentative, Benjamin now starts to say what's really bothering him:

'The world is too loud for me – too speedy – I don't feel right in this time. I'm not sure if I was born too early or too late. But I'm sure this isn't my time. I don't find my friends here. I don't find myself. I feel completely homeless. I don't know where I belong, I can't find the purpose in anything, nor adults to talk to about this calmly.

You can't cope with conflict, are always close to the end of your strength, and don't really see us at all.'

Hard to take – but the truth is always a bit painful.

What's needed today is not to make young people into a contemporary problem but to work together with them to tackle the questions and problems of our time.

Together with young people we must pose the question of ego activity and responsibility, in order to really grasp the problem of human incapacity and manipulation resulting from strictures and forces at work in society. This is the only way of activating a sense of responsibility in young people – which is actually far more present than we often imagine.

The parents speak

The mother:

Benjamin was already very hyperactive as an infant. We turned to various therapies and treatments to try to support him, so that he might find a little more inner calm and peace. He was continually aware of everything in his surroundings. He used to get very enthusiastic about everything, and then just as quickly pass on to the next thing.

I had read that hyperactive children have a particular affinity with drugs, but didn't really think any more about it – it simply wasn't an issue we thought could relate to our family.

All that changed in a moment when Benjamin was 14. His behaviour and manner suddenly became quite different from before. His former interest in everything was replaced by indifference, and he often felt bored. The openness he had shown for everything in the past turned to reticence, later even to fearfulness. This change suddenly brought home to me the fact that Benjamin was taking drugs. I felt someone had thrown a bucket of ice-cold water over me, but didn't want to ignore what was happening.

After initially denying it, Benjamin admitted regularly taking hashish.

Hoping to get advice we took him to a drugs counselling centre. Our disappointment and dismay were great when, in Benjamin's presence, we were told that as parents we simply would not be able to prevent his drugs habit, and that we would have to change our attitude. It was obvious that these people didn't think there was much wrong with taking marijuana. They accepted it as normal, so there was little help to be gained there.

But we couldn't and wouldn't leave it at that. This drug had already entered too deeply into Benjamin's state of mind and altered him. From now on I did what I could to get information on the effects of different drugs. I wanted to know the signs to watch for in Benjamin. The fact that he now took his younger sister fully into his confidence showed to what extent he himself felt out of his depth with this whole situation.

The time soon came when he no longer had enough money to finance this 'lifestyle'. When I discovered that Benjamin had simply been taking the money he needed from me, my trust was shattered. Never before had I needed to lock something away from another person; and my mistrust of him was a continual aspect of our relationship from then on. At the time this was one of the most painful moments I had ever experienced.

As time went by I learned to discuss every problem openly with Benjamin, and to enlist his help in seeking solutions. That was the sole help I could give him: the way I behaved could show him the wide gap between his actions and the mutual agreements we had made. I could prevent nothing, but at least I could be a guiding force.

Although he repeatedly took the opportunity of speaking to me about his concerns and problems, he also became increasingly aggressive towards me – to such an extent that I sometimes had the feeling that his eyes were pouring pure hatred at me. My way of talking openly to him about everything must have been like a red rag to a bull.

Thankfully the slender thread of our connection to one another never completely broke throughout this time!

What repeatedly astonished me in all these years was Benjamin's openness for conversations, therapies etc. He never refused to participate. To what extent such conversations with teachers, therapists etc. bore fruit depended on how honest people were with him, for he was always very sensitive to such things. I remember a meeting – about whether he could continue at school – where we were struggling to find some opportunity for him to have a breather and find new perspectives. There was no movement at all until everyone there dropped their masks and, as human beings rather than teacher, psychologist, counsellor, parents, entered honestly into the situation.

The most difficult times were when Benjamin lost aim and direction, and could translate into reality very little of what he had undertaken to do. He had repeatedly shown that he could do this. The decisive thing, though, was that he himself had to really want it. Then he could gather all his abilities and strength and attain what he set out to – something that always astonished us, which we would hardly have thought possible. Those were the little glimpses of light at the end of the tunnel, which kept our hope up and gave us courage to continue.

The father:

When I think back over the past 18 years since Benjamin was born, the first thing that comes to mind are the countless stress situations between Benjamin and myself, also with other members of the family and with those around him. The past has left definite scars. Constant confrontations with Benjamin – especially since the onset of puberty and the beginning of his drug habit – have had a bad effect on the whole mood of the family. Continual irritability seems to have become the norm: we often react too aggressively to one another, and in tones of voice that probably cannot become gentler again as long as Benjamin lives under one roof with us. In the past Benjamin has always found ways and means of creating this mood among us.

It gets to me when I see that in many ways I became incapable of structuring our family life in the way I wanted. Nor could my wife. The various situations with and around Benjamin often left no room for anything except reacting, and exhausting, time-consuming 'repair work'. And so often my wife and I were in total disagreement about the best way of dealing with these situations.

But at the time the issue of drugs raised its head in our family we sought help wherever we could find it, with the clear aim of safeguarding our son from addiction. In seeking 'possible solutions', as we adults call it, we had a variety of very different experiences.

Benjamin had a delicate constitution from birth: he was often fidgety and nervous, didn't like playing alone but always needed someone else to play with.

Benjamin's poor physical state meant that my wife had to carry out an extremely demanding course of physiotherapy with him only a few weeks after he was born. It was agony – for us too – each time. But it must be at least partly due to this that Benjamin is now a well-built, strong young man.

Benjamin didn't much enjoy his time at school. You could sum it up as the 'drama of the intelligent child'. A good deal of curative eurythmy[6] and regular painting therapy sessions were needed to keep him on track.

He was under-stretched by the curriculum offered in his class, and despite everyone's best efforts it did not prove possible to sufficiently compensate for this. Unfortunately his physical development at this time was still so delayed that we couldn't possibly have agreed to move him up a class.

In class Benjamin made up for his boredom by clowning about and outbursts against fellow pupils and teachers. It is true that his social behaviour in crisis situations was always exemplary. However the fact that he could take the lead was a mixed blessing, as he was also the origin of many pranks and sometimes real mischief that the many companions drawn to him carried out at his behest.

Under these circumstances it was clear that Benjamin would gradually fall behind academically. His natural intelligence was, in the end, no substitute for continuous learning. Yet he still does not seem to have understood this. On the contrary, I think that he believes the 'high intelligence' he is so often said to have means that everything ought to fall into his lap without any effort on his part.

The adults around Benjamin were often nonplussed by his extreme, aggressive reactions which surfaced when he noticed that they weren't really taking him seriously. He developed very sensitive antennae for adults who didn't give him an 'honest' answer. He mercilessly uncovered such shortcomings and used his verbal skills to nail them to the wall.

I well remember the time when the situation at school had got so out of hand that the only possible way forward was for Benjamin to leave. He handled the change to state secondary school fine as far as curriculum and social integration were concerned – but that's when another 'subject' began to preoccupy his attention: first cigarette smoking. And then, via a group of friends whom we parents could soon no longer keep tabs on, drugs as well.

Drinking sessions with much older kids from the village were our greatest worry for a while, for we knew that Benjamin would not only 'try out' everything going, but would also (as he himself always admitted) do it to excess.

Benjamin assured us again and again that he was 'in control' of his drugs habit. He knew, he said, what was good for him. He had already tried everything, and the substance he was using at the moment was proven to have no harmful physical or mental effects.

We soon found out how much he was deceiving himself when patterns emerged that can only be described as severe weakness of will. He made many theoretical plans but was almost incapable of realising them. Many of his motor skills and abilities have since gone by the board. Periods of all-night carousing with his mates alternate with deep depressions, during which problems arise which seem to him insoluble. He lacks all inner motivation to change this pattern. He continually swings between totally overdoing things and wretched misery.

One moment he's the absolutely cool dude who thinks he and others can take on the world – the next he's a picture of misery and anxiety, who can see no way out of a situation when he feels it's got on top of him.

It is a fact that most parents are helpless, unable to do anything for their adolescents when faced with such situations. The widespread ignorance of many adults who simply do not want to see how close to home the drug problem is, is staggering! Others, in contrast, who have more awareness of the drugs problem, seem to me to be far too unconcerned about the whole subject.

One thing I have come to see is that we adults are up against a development in the lives of young people which we still judge by old traditional standards, since we lack any new means of dealing with it. This probably means we aren't doing the best for young people. And they're right when they say that despite our theoretical 'improvements' to the modern world, the reality is that we're helpless in the face of the smallest problems.

I'm no better myself. With my no doubt old-fashioned value judge-ments, I simply wasn't able to properly judge the scene around my son. So I was, and still am, unable to meet it with the right understanding – a fact that leaves me in a painfully helpless situation.

What remains is the hope that Benjamin will one day be able to free himself from the mental straitjacket of drugs without sustaining too much physical damage. There are some faint signs of this, but for me they are the light at the end of the tunnel.

I think that Benjamin probably ought to leave home and take himself and his own life in hand.

But I'm still left with many questions:

Does time really heal all wounds? I don't think so. How many young people never get out of the scene! What did I do wrong? What am I still doing wrong? What am I doing at all? Basically all I did was find as stress-free a way of living with Benjamin as possible, but I know that's no solution. But is there a solution at all?

These open, unadorned accounts, for which I am very grateful, show how inappropriately we adults usually tackle young people's drug habits, and how inappropriately young people themselves regard their own habit.

How frequently we encounter two opposite stances to this problem, that either play down drug consumption as harmless, or build it up into an enormous problem. Both approaches show how far away we are from seeing drug-taking not as a failure but as a challenge to us to focus our awareness and interest on young people.

What we really need to ask is how to re-engender vital and supportive relationships with young people, and whether it is possible for us to help them through the situation they find themselves in, or whether therapeutic help needs to be sought elsewhere.

We can see how far the drug-taker himself is from making a proper assessment of his habit and its effect from what Benjamin said to his father:

He was in control of his drug habit, he said; he knew what was good for him; the substance he was taking had no bad physical or mental effects.

Such statements are especially typical of hashish consumers, and show to what extent the drug can undermine their perception and assessment of themselves.

1 Jacques Lusseyran: *Against the Pollution of the I,* Parabola Books; ISBN: 0930407466

2 Quoted in *Weisst du, dass die Bäume reden – Weisheit der Indianer,* Freiburg i. Br. 1998

3 Gender will alternate from chapter to chapter, to avoid any unintended impression that this book is prejudiced towards either a masculine or feminine view of things (translator's note)

4 Quoted in the magazine *Erziehungskunst,* no. 4 (1998)

5 ibid

6 A form of movement taught in Rudolf Steiner (Waldorf) schools

*Everything that liberates the spirit
without giving us self-mastery
is pernicious*

J.W.von Goethe

2

Addiction – ego entrapment

Drugs and their effects

The abuse of addictive substances represents one of the chief psycho-social and health problems in Germany. Tobacco and alcohol occupy first and second places in the spectrum of most frequently misused addictive substances, followed by sedative and analgesic medicines, hashish, heroin, ecstasy and amphetamines.

A closer examination of high-risk, abusive and dependent drug use is needed to arrive at a differentiated picture of the epidemiological consequences of the consumption of various substances. A differentiated survey is an important precondition for the development of an integrated support system: from prevention and early intervention, damage-limiting and health-stabilising measures, through to further development of support for coming off drugs and social integration.

As part of the representative survey on drug use in Germany (government study by the Federal Health Ministry), the 1997 survey for the first time provides us with statistics of clinically relevant groups of drug users in Germany (Kraus & Bauernfeind, 1998; Kraus, Bauernfeind & Bühringer, 1998). The following figures for alcohol abuse apply to people aged between 18 and 59 (18-69):

Total high-risk consumption	16%	7.8 million	(9.3 million)
of which abusive consumption	5%	2.4 million	(2.7 million)
of which addictive consumption	3%	1.5 million	(1.7 million)[1]

Drug dependency

Drugs change our consciousness. They do this in very different ways according to the nature of the various substances.

Drugs are toxic substances or poisons that have a direct effect on the central nervous system and thus influence our state of consciousness. The organism's natural defences which, when a substance is first taken, lead to vomiting, headache, cramps, restlessness and fears, are weakened and put out of action when a consumer repeatedly takes the toxic substance in order to recreate a desired change of consciousness. As drug-use continues our bodily defences come less and less into play, but at the same time the mind-altering power of the drug is also reduced. This is the start of a vicious circle in which the user strives at all costs for a state of consciousness mediated by the drug. The dose must continually increase in order to attain the same effect. After initially defending itself against the toxic substance, the body gradually gets used to it, so that its reaction undergoes a reversal: it objects more and more strongly when it no longer receives the substance. The consumer shows withdrawal symptoms, which initially manifest in a rather similar way to the body's original defence reactions, but which can then intensify in the mental/ emotional realm to hallucinations and deep depressions. At this stage of drug consumption we speak of dependency or addiction – in other words the organism no longer functions normally unless it obtains a certain dose of the drug substance.

For millennia human beings have taken drugs. In former cultures they were used during religious rituals, in order to enable those who had prepared for this through rigorous spiritual training to gain spiritual insights. The community needed such insight and illumination, which was then placed at its disposal without desire for personal gain. In those times drug use was never self-focused.

Other drug substances, such as opium and cannabis, have been used from ancient times as medicines and remedies.

At the beginning of the 19th century the opium-derived substance morphine was discovered and used in medicine.

Around the turn of the last century the pharmaceutical industry created a whole series of psychotropic ('mind-affecting') substances, including heroin, as chemical derivatives of morphine. People hoped that heroin would prove to be a powerful analgesic without addictive qualities – a tragic mistake as became apparent during the first decades of the twentieth century.

After the second world war, a broad spectrum of drugs developed very rapidly – and also a wide network of dealers.

Numerous new medicines came onto the market, especially the benzodiazepam preparations still in use as sleeping medicines and tranquillisers.

In the middle of the last century LSD (lysergic acid diethylamide) was discovered as a mind-altering drug. Taking it was said to expand consciousness – a promise which led many to use it during the sixties. Consumption of a substance to relax the mind and feel 'good' also began in the sixties with cannabis, which became widespread as the hippy drug.

Drug consumption with the aim of altering consciousness became more and more common during the seventies and eighties and led to a growing assortment of substances with various effects. Currently the trend is mainly towards activity-enhancing and euophoria-creating substances such as cocaine, amphetamines, ecstasy and other designer drugs.

The effect of different drugs[2]

Nicotine

Desired experience: increased concentration, calming down, getting distance from things, having another try at something, having a real break for a moment and coming back to oneself, overcoming sleepiness, being able to stay awake longer.

Some consequences for health: heart problems, headaches, disease of the respiratory organs, increased risk of cancer, poor peripheral circulation. Smokers are particularly at risk of circulatory and cancer illnesses.

Alcohol

Desired experience: socialising, speaking freely to others, leaving daily cares behind, being happy and relaxed, creating a festive atmosphere, finding comfort when lonely.

Physical effects:

Phase 1: stimulating, enlivening, warming

Phase 2: increasing activity, loquaciousness, euphoria

Phase 3: intoxication and weakening of thinking and sense perception

Some consequences for health: loss of memory, brain damage, liver illness, kidney damage, muscle tremor, raised blood pressure, sleeping disorders, sweating, nerve paralysis, illnesses of the pancreas, alcoholic embryopathy (harming of the child in the womb), testicular atrophy resulting in sterility and impotence.

Cannabis and its products marijuana and hashish (from the female hemp plant)

Effects induced after a few minutes when smoked, length of effect 2-10 hours, active ingredient THC (Tetrahydrocannabinol).

Desired experience: standing above the daily strictures of habits, duties, deadlines, stress and annoyance; feeling high; feeling happy, free and uncompelled, and being able to laugh about everything;

experiencing thoughts, feelings and sense perceptions, also time and space, in a quite new and different way from ordinary daily life – more elemental, beyond normal conditions, in new perspectives; experiencing all this 'consciously' in a dreamy state between waking and sleeping.

Some consequences for health: Changes to sense perception, reduced capacity to concentrate and learn, smaller number of sperm cells, irregularity of the female cycle, developmental disorders in unborn children, weakening of the immune system.

Ecstasy (XTC) and other designer drugs (combinations of amphetamines, ephedrines and caffeine in a nutmeg oil-base, so-called saffron oil)

XTC tablets are especially high-risk because they often contain additional substances such as LSD etc.

Desired experience: changes to feeling life, being able to open up and show feelings, lessening of fear, increased readiness to talk with and relate to others; intuitively experiencing how the other is feeling, getting rid of inhibitions of all kinds; totally 'outing' oneself – showing feelings just as they are, uninhibited and direct.

Some consequences for health: feeling exhausted and drained, pounding heart, insomnia, disorientation, anxiety, hallucinations, depressions, release of serotonin leading to synapse stress and irreversible biochemical processes.

LSD / lysergic acid diathylamide / ergot alkaloids

LSD works even in small quantities of a ten-thousandth of a gram, and is therefore embedded in other, container materials: e.g. blotting paper with comic designs.

The effect begins after roughly 30-45 minutes, and lasts between 7 and 12 hours. The trip is very much connected with one's mental state and surroundings. Sense reversals appear: colours are heard and tones seen. A risk involved in LSD consumption is the 'horror trip' in which fear and panic seem to go on endlessly. There is danger of severe accidents or suicide through misjudging situations ('I can fly').

Desired experience: out-of-body experiences, coloured visions and hallucinations; experiences of warmth and light; one's whole life unfolding in a panorama; resurfacing of long-forgotten memories and experiences; being centred in oneself yet at the same time out of oneself in another world.

Some consequences for health: passing psychotic states, delusions, kidney/liver damage, residual unreliability of sense impressions, flashbacks as lingering psychoses – i.e. onset of a new intoxication effect without the drug, and sometimes weeks after the drug was taken.

Cocaine and amphetamines

The effect begins swiftly and lasts only a short while, especially with cocaine.

Risk of: quickly developing dependency with collapse into a deep depression.

Desired experience: experiencing oneself as strong and capable, and above all unusually clear, quick-thinking and decisive; longing for spiritual exertion and stimulus, for what is very special, for a grandiose sense of self-worth and superiority compared with everyone else; orgiastic feeling of blissful happiness; a sense of unlimited physical powers, of being able to overstep the normal boundaries of tiredness; being wakeful and strong.

Some consequences for health: headaches, stomach cramps, feelings of dizziness, pounding heart, insomnia, irritability, feeling restless and driven, fear.

Heroin, opium and its most important constituent morphine (morpheus = god of sleep) and other opiates

This substance is usually injected, though often smoked as well.

The effect begins swiftly and lasts for 3-5 hours.

Desired experience: Deep peace, being relaxed and able to sleep despite pain and worry; experiencing oneself as free and light, lifted out of the body, as a lightly floating being, that can become one with surrounding light, colour and other beings; longing for eternal peace and sleep; darkness, annihilation of consciousness in comforting warmth; being 'in paradise', experiencing something close to an after-death state in a world of spirit; euphoric joy and bliss without feeling held back by the heaviness of the body or daily cares; longing for the 'flash' which frees one in a moment from life's narrow straits, from daily greyness and mundanity, from pedestrian ways of thought.

Some consequences for health: heroin is highly addictive but gives rise to the least actual physical damage. The following symptoms are common through failing to eat and unsafe injecting: weakening of the digestive system, inhibition of sexual functions, muscle cramps, pale skin, emaciation, limbs and joints becoming stiff and clumsy; ultimately the ruin of all bodily functions, physical degeneration, hepatitis infections, AIDS.

Risk: swift development of physical dependency with strong physical withdrawal symptoms.

All drugs that are misused involve damage to health in the sense of premature ageing and increasing loss of ego: in other words ego activity disorders and loss of self-control at a physical, mental and spiritual level.

Why drugs? Motives and risks

First we need to distinguish between experimental use and regular consumption which can become excessive use and dependency. The phase of initial and experimental use often begins at about the age of 13 or 14, and in exceptional cases as young as 11 or 12. In this phase curiosity is the prime factor, the desire for new experiences and the frisson of danger. Using drugs is also, above all, a way of separating oneself from a society which rejects young people. Quite often this first taste of drugs is also linked to the hope of dealing better with, or cutting out, daily stress situations, and escaping from a far too loud and hectic world (see Benjamin's story, page 12). From occasional use regular use can quickly develop. The drug-user only rarely notices when consumption starts to rule her life. Drugs help to relax, stimulate and comfort: they reveal a desired world. But the moment that the drug wears off, daily life becomes greyer, more boring, flat or stressful; and then the vicious circle begins which leads to ever-increasing drug use.

Another important motive for drug consumption is the wish to alleviate mental/emotional problems (sexual abuse for instance), to 'treat' them if you like. These accompanying disorders are often a decisive factor in the development of addiction.

Every form of deterrent strategy as part of drugs education is ineffective for young people. (The best way to teach them is through our own example. Overcoming our own addictive habits can have a definite, indirect influence on them.) Yet the generally known and widely experienced negative effects of drugs do need to be cited and repeatedly emphasised. The degree of damage incurred by drug use naturally depends on many different factors: which drugs are used, how, in what amounts, how often, and by which individual.[3] At the same time it is also necessary to distinguish between acute risks during drug use and subsequent consequences manifesting sometimes years or decades later.

One thing that must be stressed is the great danger of accidents, for all drugs alter sense perception and our ability to react to the outer world. In addition a willingness to take risks surfaces, which the drug-user herself cannot properly assess.

A second major problem is overdosing on a drug. Fatal

poisoning through an overdose is not exceptional. Intoxicating substances can lead to an unexpected arrest of all life functions. The respiratory centre can be paralysed, and stimulants can lead to a collapse of the over-stimulated heart and circulatory system.

The combination of several drugs is particularly dangerous (polytoxicity). Many drug-users who have drunk alcohol and smoked cannabis at the same time report the appearance of unpredictable mood swings, dizzy fits and so-called hash-psychoses. This symptom is increasing drastically at the moment. Dependency on a single substance is fairly rare at the peak stage of a drug-user's 'career'.

There are a number of drugs which involve the risk of physical dependency, though this is not the prime danger of drug-use. Physical addiction occurs when the organism becomes habituated to the drug substance. Continual use leads to down-regulation of brain receptors, so that lack of the drug leads to physical malfunctions, experienced as withdrawal symptoms such as restlessness, aggression, sweating, circulatory disorders, collapse etc. But mental/emotional dependency is present with *all* drugs. This is the overpowering desire to take the drug to sustain the level of mood that one has previously experienced through it. 'Mental' withdrawal can sometimes take years, and is the real problem of drug-use.

This explains why hashish taken regularly over many years can be more dangerous than heroin, whose destructive effect becomes obvious far more rapidly, and is therefore easier to take seriously. Hashish on the other hand can be dismissed as harmless for a long time, since it is only after a long period that anyone – particularly the user herself – notices the dangers and damage it causes.

Recent research has shown that the main active ingredient in hashish, THC, is stored in the body for weeks, and during this time can take sudden and unexpected effect. This can lead to the 'flashbacks' that are rightly feared, and their unquantifiable deficiency symptoms in the brain. It has also been shown that

THC attacks genetic material, seriously weakens the immune system, slows down stress hormone activity in the brain, paralyses self-awareness and critical faculties, causes emotional deficiencies which can extend to psychoses of a kind more and more frequently observed. Typical consequences for social behaviour are the breakdown of existing relationships, the limitation of social contact to others in the hashish-scene, as well as a general lack of interest in everything that is not directly linked with this.

1   From *Jahrbuch der Sucht 2000*
2   For a more comprehensive description of drugs and their effects, see books such as *How Drugs Work* and *Drugfax* listed under 'Further Reading'
3   For instance, a heroin overdose is more likely to occur if the drug is injected rather than being swallowed

I well understand why so many young people turn to drugs.
Let me assure you that I fully understand why they wish to draw a veil over this world, in which whole populations or great forests are destroyed every day, and in which persecutions can be accomplished in cold-blooded intellect.

Jacques Lusseyran

3

Social isolation and its consequences

Stefan

Lonely wanderings
The rain streams
ice-cold down my neck.
I feel bad and weak.
There's no one else on the road,
no one as far as the eye can see.
I just hear the wind and rain howling.
I'm close to freezing from the cold all around me.
But on I walk into eternity.

Stefan, 16 years old[1]

In former times people always felt themselves to be part of a community that provided safety and security, in which they felt protected and for which they felt responsible.

Think of the old-fashioned extended family – with, say, grandparents, and an aunt and uncle living under one roof, all taking a share in bringing up the children. In those days each individual was very much formed by family consciousness, a consciousness of social position which offered clear rules of behaviour. This social protection no longer exists. In this age of individual freedom from group norms and higher authorities we are at the same time living without the security that these things offer. Our sense of ego, however much in its infancy it may still be, is linked with the experience of loneliness and crisis. This is a developmental phase involving darkness, painful knowledge and breakdowns. Attempts to flee the loneliness and restrictions of this evolutionary situation frequently look to drugs for help.

Yet we need courage to endure this zero point.

'I well understand why so many young people turn to drugs. Let me assure you that I fully understand why they wish to draw a veil over this world, in which whole populations or great forests are destroyed every day, and in which persecutions do not occur in frenzy but in cold-blooded intellect. Indeed, how can one long endure this civilisation in which the soul is hemmed in, straitjacketed, labelled and insulted? How can one take pleasure in a society in which imagination will soon have no function except for leisure activities? And in which people try only to measure everything, even happiness, just as one weighs artificial fertiliser or cement. I fully understand that they are moved by one wish alone – to get away from it. But when they leave, do they arrive anywhere? They ought to be told that they will not arrive!…'

Jacques Lusseyran[2]

To acknowledge and affirm crises nowadays is truly difficult – in a time when swift solutions, conflict-avoidance strategies and the 'easy way out' have become the norm.

Acknowledging and affirming crises means accepting a sense of powerlessness, allowing breakdowns to happen, being willing to undergo painful processes, and overcoming comfortable concepts and ideas which have become too fixed and rigid.

Nowadays, instead, we often experience media-addiction, poverty of communication, predictable encounters in the 'chat-room', and illusory meetings under the intoxicating influence of drugs.

'I well understand'

Intentional use of certain substances can, it is true, give the illusion of presence of mind, light, warmth, real communication, safety in the world, feelings of concentration and simultaneous relaxation – but these experiences and emotions occur without the core of the personality, the ego; they are a substitute for it and actually suppress your true being.

One soul only develops real warmth with another.

Only true meeting between people engenders the warmth which nourishes the soul, through which they can develop further.

Lea

Do you hear my thoughts, friend?
The thunder rolls
Behind my forehead
Surely you hear it?
Surging thoughts
Torture me
Crying I give them voice
Thundering waves roll
Over my lips
Can't you hear them?

Lea, 15 years old[3]

Ecstasy

After about 15-20 minutes it begins: this tingling in my body, you can't move your arms and legs freely any more, your heart suddenly starts beating faster, and then you float off. I feel nothing but warmth, I'm completely relaxed, cool, I let myself go, I'd like to sink away with someone, touch and sense someone. I feel warmth, an amazing feeling, totally relaxed. With ecstasy you can completely get inside someone else's skin, everything gets bright around you, you feel sympathy for everything and everyone, total empathy. It's a crazy feeling of peace – you're one with yourself, with the world, you feel there's purpose, you feel light and clarity, you feel love.

Lena, 17 years old[4]

Ecstasy, MDMA, methylenedioxymethamphetamine. The effect of ecstasy comes from a combination of the effects of hash and speed. The mind is driven in two directions at once. Part of the soul is as though physically inhaled, the other part is dissolved into the wider world, giving a strong sense of one's environment. All experiences and feelings are enormously intensified by means of ecstasy. The broadening out and extending of one's emotional life leads to a sense of great intimacy with everything: sympathy, sense of community, feelings of love.

Part of MDMA has an effect similar to LSD, i.e. a trip becomes possible in which the life forces are separated from the body, so that one experiences a death-process type release from the physical – pure spiritual experience. The stimulant part of ecstasy creates the urge to move. Incredible physical energy is released through dancing.

There are side-effects such as a feeling of sickness, shivering (similar to flu), states of anxiety, sweating, tiredness, depression, headache, sense of emptiness, extreme perspiration. Possible long-term effects are: loss of appetite, lack of motivation or will, extreme irritability and unwelcome hallucinations.

The experience of relaxation, solution, warmth, love, well-being, connectedness with everything and everyone that ecstasy offers – albeit only in a biochemical and illusionary way – can show us what we need to work for in the social sphere. Nowadays life is increasingly experienced as a frantic whirl. We are continually confronted by the new and unexpected. More and more people go travelling, seek a new place to live, change their jobs or find no work. We do not have the emotional equipment to deal with our rapid pace of life, and feel more and more uprooted and homeless. Unemployment, all kinds of pressure, collapsing social systems – all these things nowadays make us timid, speechless and cold.

Parents have less time for their children than ever before. According to a statistical survey, a mother allows an average of twelve minutes per day for real, non purpose-driven conversation with her child.

Let's take time!

Eleven-year-old Morten is incurably ill and is going to die. He writes a very sober and honest letter to Simon, a journalist, in which he describes how lonely a child can feel, and how illness has totally changed his situation. This letter is printed in the newspaper, and unleashes an avalanche of letters from children and adults about cares, worries, illness and death, but also about joy, hope and friendship.

Here is an extract from Morten's letter:

In the past I would probably have told you that I don't feel too good, or that I'm lonely. I especially felt like that at home. Mum and Dad always had so much to do, they worked and worked. I'm an only child and mostly I was alone. I got quite a few presents – none of my friends had as much as me. Yes, of course I wanted all these things. But I would have preferred to spend more time enjoying being together at home. I was fairly good at school, and my parents were very proud about this. They said I was intelligent, and I was just the kind of boy they would have wished for. So there was no lack of praise. But then I became very ill, over a year ago; and now here's the good thing about my illness: suddenly things were very different with Mum, Dad and me. They were with me nearly the whole time, or at least one of them was.. And they often told me how much they loved me. They hardly ever used to say that before. I'd never given it much thought either, but now I did, afterwards. I realised that I hadn't believed that they loved me in the least, before I became ill.[5]

Nowadays there are many children and young people who feel themselves to be superfluous and unwanted in this world. The wound of their unwantedness injures them in their depths. Children whose family life is marked by social coldness, sense very early in their lives an unquenchable longing for protection and warmth – an ideal gateway for drugs and their effects.

Evenings where people do things together, with conversations and stories told at the dinner table, are on the decline. People just gather round the television and take what food they want from the fridge, whenever each person wants. A sense of shared community in which all are connected is becoming increasingly rare.

Social isolation needs the remedy of social warmth. If the soul needing real meeting, and warm interest and attention, can only get this on a physical level, through substances, then these are optimal conditions for addiction to take root. Addiction always surfaces when real fulfilment cannot occur.

When you take heroin you feel the sun's rising inside you. It warms you inside, warms everything. It's crazy. There's nothing like it.

Christian

1 Quoted in: Thomas Stöckli – *Jugendpädagogik. Was tun?*, Dornach 1998

2 From A*gainst the Pollution of the 'I'*

3 See note 1

4 See note 1

5 Simon Flem Devold: *Morten, 11 Jahre. Gespräche mit einem sterbenden Kind*, Stuttgart 1998

Life!
My life!
Without collar and lead,
No unnecessary restrictions,
No limits,
Guidelines perhaps,
I'm allowed to enjoy it;
Either scarcely,
Or to the full.
I have that right!
There's one thing only you can't deny me:
Freedom!

poem by a sixteen year old[1]

4

Addiction and ego development

Human evolution

In former times human beings experienced themselves as an integral part of their surroundings, and as living in the present moment.

During the centuries awareness gradually awoke of self and the world as distinct from one another. We increasingly saw ourselves as separate beings who conquered nature through thinking. This evolution reached its peak in modern times, in which we now experience ourselves as free individuals able to create our own biography. But the more we experience ourselves as free, the more lonely we are too. This is the cause of today's addiction phenomenon. Ego consciousness and freedom are accompanied by the other side of the coin – tendencies to addiction and dependency.

At the turn of the 21st century the ego has been torn out of traditional social circumstances; it wishes only to depend on itself and be free – but at the same time it experiences itself as vulnerable, uncertain and open to attack.

Every crisis – a word which in fact derives from 'judgement' and 'decision' – starts from a process of growing lonely. And in this loneliness we experience our focus on an ego power that is still nourished wholly from the past. This is the aspect of us which unthinkingly claims rights and advantages over others, a power that was necessary for the evolution of personality but which now isolates us more and more. The connecting, warming aspect of the 'I', which is present in all of us, needs to liberate itself from this outdated egotism. This is the aspect of ego power which opens us to the other and allows us to develop helping and empathising qualities.

'Our ego is this desire we all have not to be exactly the same as everyone else; and, whatever the price, to stand out in some way… in whatever way it might be. This monstrous desire to capture a greater part of the booty for ourselves, to be in the right even when we're wrong, is produced by the ego: ambition, competitiveness… the fanaticism, the authoritarianism which one would like to dress up as true authority. The ego is this force that seeks to alienate us from each other… it is the illness of non-communication, of autism… The death sentence and poison of the ego is that the more we only become ourselves, the more we will be alone. All are striving for the ego, this treacherous part of our 'I'… but they all forget that the ego is not the 'I' but only its fleeting, shifting momentary surface, and that one destroys the 'I' when one accords the ego every right. The 'I' is fragile. None of us even really possess it… it is like an impulse, a kind of momentum… a power that it still very close to its birth. The ego needs things, the largest possible number of things. Whether these things are money, recognition, mastery, applause or reward, the 'I' does not have any interest in it. The 'I' is wealth in the midst of poverty. It is the interest when everything is bored around me. It is the hope even when all objective chances seem to have vanished. And ultimately it is what remains when everything else has been taken away, when nothing more comes towards us from

> outside; and yet our powers are great enough to overcome this emptiness.'
>
> Jacques Lusseyran[2]

If we open ourselves to the path of development involved in strengthening this selfless aspect of our 'I', then we will have to face crises, leave behind old, comfortable certainties and undergo death processes of the soul. Drug-users experience this death too, but they do it without their 'I'. Thus these experiences cannot have a consciousness-waking effect.

Acknowledging crises

Loneliness, fears, feeling powerless, death processes – these are one aspect of contemporary experience. Having the courage to endure these zero points without avoiding them, without turning to intoxicants, is a prerequisite for further inner development towards consciousness, freedom and responsibility. Only when we develop readiness to relinquish old certainties and supports and at the same time accept the powerlessness which accompanies this, can a space arise for something new, for something of the present which is not determined by the past, for presence of mind.

For our ego-fixation to dissolve, processes of suffering need to open us up. If we do not learn, in overcoming old concepts and conditions, to endure death processes in the mental and emotional realm, drugs will gain an increasing power of attraction. Then, instead of these death processes being undergone in the soul and spirit, in conscious zero-point experiences, they are transferred into the physical realm where the drug has a destructive effect on the body and its life forces. Illusionary spiritual experiences arise, without the participation of our true ego forces.

Addiction has become a question of culture, civilisation and 'I'.

This question arises at the same level as those relating to death, birth, health and evolution.

The question of addiction is *the* great question of our times, and is as multi-faceted as these times. Therefore we cannot solve the question and problem of addiction with short-term measures or get a grip on it with fixed programmes.

> Suffering is a phenomenon that accompanies higher development. It is an unavoidable and irreplaceable part of knowledge.
> Rudolf Steiner[3]

More and more people are distancing themselves from external 'norms' and trying to take responsibility for their lives. The first steps have already been taken towards an individual life lived through self-reliant powers of judgement.

On this path towards freedom we have to face our own inner world: and here live fears, traumas, wounds and injuries. It is not easy to live with them – but it does bring its rewards.

Addiction's many faces

In the last decades the problem of addiction has become one of the most central cultural problems. When we speak of addiction in this book, this does not refer only to drugs but to addiction in general.

What is addiction? One possible definition:

Addiction is an intensifying, compulsive process in which conflicts are suppressed through any kind of outer stimulation, and replaced by enjoyment without self-exertion.

This definition shows clearly that we live in an addictive society nowadays – for who among us has not experienced actions which take on a life of their own, which remove us from conscious, 'I'-based direction and threaten to become compulsive? For instance there are process-linked addictions preceded by a long phase of habituation, such as TV addiction, computer addiction, internet dependency (now accepted by WHO as a recognised illness), games addiction, work addiction, relationship addiction, criticism addiction, sex addiction. A further level of addiction is that involving foods or substances commonly enjoyed in daily life: eating addiction, anorexia, bulimia, nicotine addiction, alcohol addiction. Finally we have the level of substance addiction which includes all drugs such as cocaine, crack, LSD, alcohol, opiates, ecstasy, designer drugs of the most varied kinds, psychotropic drugs and other medicines.

If we now examine the numbers of people with a dependency problem, this last level has the smallest number of consumers, but receives greatest attention from the media.

Underlying all forms of addiction is an unquenchable longing for peace, protection, purpose and certainty. These are states which were formerly provided as a matter of course by people's place within fixed, social forms. Nowadays each individual has to attain them alone. The fact that we all struggle with poor self-esteem is therefore not surprising; nor is the power of attraction of substances which appear to offer self-awareness, enhanced ability to communicate, purposefulness and joy. If we understand what is going on here and take a critical look at ourselves, we have to acknowledge that we all tend towards certain forms of addiction. If we can find the will and courage to observe ourselves dispassionately, all desire to moralise and judge addicts will fade. Instead we will become far more ready to understand and try to help.

It is this very readiness which our young people really need from us nowadays, so as to avoid ever falling into dependency in the first place.

What leads to addiction?

Are there particular dispositions which lead to dependency? Can one discover an 'addictive personality' already in early childhood?

This question cannot be answered so simply. *The* addictive personality, family or single cause does not exist – instead there is a combination of different factors at work. One has to examine each person's individual biography to find the answers, for addiction is always a many-layered story.

Dependency or addiction is a condition that we are all susceptible to nowadays. Simple explanations or even the apportioning of blame are of no help. There are often underlying situations of emotional distress which have not been fully worked through or dealt with, such as:

- lack of love and protection in childhood, including violence and mental, sexual or physical abuse
- parents' unemployment
- parents' separation
- death of a loved one
- stress arising from poverty and lack of support (e.g. a single-parent situation)

People are much more liable to be sucked in to addiction if they have felt themselves unloved and unwanted from infancy onwards. It is difficult to develop healthy self-awareness if, instead of learning to cope with conflicts in the family and make sense of them, one only learns mechanisms of suppression. If such children then find that drugs provide exactly what they are lacking in their lives, they will be in real danger of falling prey to them.

Today's society makes us human beings lonely – and addiction makes us still lonelier.

'I want to follow my star...'

I see now that there is a past behind me and a future before me. I look back on a history that is mine, and before me open unknown paths. Only one thing seems clear: I will take one step after another and each step continues my story. I am afraid of this uncertainty. But then I feel full of confidence again when I think that this is my life, my future which I myself wish to form in my own way. But where does this all lead ultimately? Where and how does it begin? Why does it begin at all? When I look back I come to a point where memory is extinguished. Before this point is darkness, nothing. Or am I wrong? People say to me: You're old enough to learn that in the far-distant future there's another such point, where everything stops and grows dark. People just have to live with it. And was that how things were before my life began? Nothing to start with, nothing in the end, and in between some story or other that's supposed to give everything sense and purpose? What do I care for your ideas of morality, and the way you encourage me to take an active part in life, take responsibility for myself and others; for your warnings that I ought to learn, strive, make myself useful – is that all you can tell me? Don't bother me with your comfortable pieties. Old man God with the beard has no more to offer. And I really can't get on with the idea that, when people's lives are over, they return to some great, all-embracing peace where no one is any longer of any importance to themselves. Of course they aren't if they're just not there! This kind of paradise isn't any less alarming than the great black hole of nothingness. Even ornate and flowery nothings are still nothing. If the great questions are too much for you, it'd be better to admit it rather than spreading mysterious fog over everything and thinking I could lose my way in this fog in which you try to conceal your own fears...

I seek truth and honesty, I want to know whether I'm just surrounded by tired, empty individuals who have come to accept nothing on the one hand and nothing on the other, and who travel the stretch in between without knowing why, just because they have no choice. Is this the only, unavoidable consequence of what you call 'being reasonable'? Or are there any among you who haven't stopped searching, who cannot be content with the simple 'let's just get on with it' that rules people's lives; or the still less comforting God who can mean everything and nothing? I want to find people among you I can trust, whom I can ask my questions about the sense of everything, about where we come from and where we go. People who don't just sentimentally think: 'How wonderful to be so young and foolish'; or who cuttingly reply: 'Leave your dream-world behind, it'll only make you ill. Learn, work, make something of yourself and take pleasure in the wage you earn.' I want to know the meaning of the longing that has awoken in me, that burns in my body and stirs up my soul. Will it find a goal or just keep wandering aimlessly?... until it is extinguished again, as though nothing had ever been. My love longs to speak through my life, my body. This desire feels bright and good, and at the same time tastes like forbidden fruit, like danger, like a wound – as though I were trying to free something incredibly precious from the claws of a monster. I'm asking you whether my feelings are right or have I just been seized by the same natural forces which urge dogs to mate? No, I don't expect any answers, I only want to know whether there are people out there who understand the questions that move my inmost being, because they are also their own questions. Has anyone dared to grow older yet stay young? Can anyone listen to me in a way that helps me find the right words in her presence, rather than having to feel it's impossible to say what I mean, and so sending out signals all the time which seem bizarre, odd, awkward and arrogant, because no one can decipher them?

I want to follow my star. I seek other people who look at me in a way that says; 'Yes, you're right, there is such a star, it's travelling ahead of you, don't lose sight of it. I too am following my life's star – believe in it. Don't let yourself be turned aside. It may be a hard journey, but it's worth carrying on.' And if I should find such a person, she will have to be prepared to forgive me for seeming so difficult, showing so little thanks for what she gives me. As I turn to her inwardly, full of trust and relief, I will say many things that may sound as though I am rejecting her. But I hope she will understand that I am moved by shame. Shame of my own strong feelings; and shame of being so needy of someone like her being there for me...

A teenager's letter [4]

Drug-use is an integral part of our society, particularly of the adult world. Drug-use is not a youth-phenomenon but adult behaviour, imitated, like much else, by young people.

It is interesting to see what functions drug-use – particularly of illegal drugs – can have for young people. Drugs can:

- be used consciously to cause affront and hurt to the values held by society or parents;
- be used to demonstrate and anticipate adult behaviour (anticipation or negative expectation);
- be a type of excessive behaviour and typical teenage expression of a lack of self-control;
- open the way to friendships and circles of friends;
- symbolise participation in subculture lifestyles;
- be a means to resolve frustrating situations of everyday life;
- be an emergency reaction to developmental disorders/disturbances;
- be a substitute for unmanageable demands on one's own development;
- be a means of expressing unmanageable demands on one's own development;
- be a way to express social protest and criticism of social structure.[5]

1   Thomas Stöckli: *Jugendpädagogik. Was tun?* Dornach 1998
2   Jacques Lusseyran: *Against the Pollution of the 'I'.*
3   Rudolf Steiner: *Geistige Hierarchien und ihre Wiederspiegelung in der physischen Welt. Tierkreis, Planeten, Kosmos* (GA 110), lecture of 21 April 1909, Dornach 1991
4   Published in *Info3,* issue 12 (1988)
5   Klaus Hurrelman, quoted by: Rüdiger Meyenberg in *Sucht und Erziehung in der Schule,* Oldenburg 1990

Freedom in the deepest sense of the word means more
than saying what I think with no holds barred.
Freedom means that I also see the other,
that I put myself in his place
and, by sensitively grasping all this, that I am able
to extend my freedom
through empathy.
For what else is mutual understanding but
extending freedom and deepening truth.

Vaclav Havel

5

Relating today – social competence tomorrow

Do we understand our children and youngsters?

People often make out that drugs are someone else's problem. Teachers and parents often have no inkling that their own children, or pupils in their own class, are smoking dope or taking other 'introductory' drugs. Any suspicions remain in the obscure realm of rumour; and depending on their own capacity to deal with such issues, people either try to see what is going on or determinedly look away. In one class 8 parents' evening (age 13-14), parents who tried to talk about the issue of hash consumption in the class were simply admonished by the teacher with a suggestion that things were probably not quite 'right' in their own homes.

On the other hand teachers who are concerned about a pupil's obvious drug-use often find that parents block this off, not wishing to look at it, and rebuff the teacher. When one's own child takes drugs this is either felt to be a disgrace and hushed up, or regarded as normal.

Only recently a 9th-grader (age 14-15) was indignant when I spoke about the dangers of hashish use. He was, he said, very surprised by this negative view: his parents and he started each day with a breakfast joint, and this made them feel great. No one could say that his parents were trying to harm him.

What this lad does not see, because he is no longer able to, are the consequences of this 'breakfast joint', which his teachers told me about afterwards: he is enormously forgetful, doesn't keep his word, talks continually without noticing it, steamrollers over his fellows without any sense of respect, without waking up through their reactions. The parents do not make the connection with hashish consumption, but think this is poor discipline at school.

The 'normalisation' of drug-use by children and young people delivers them up solely to the laws of the drug world.

It is a fact that young people of 13 to 14, and sometimes younger, are already taking cannabis as though this was the most normal thing in the world. If you listen to young people it will very soon become clear how widespread so-called soft drugs are, and how much they have become part of normality in a way that can give us pause for thought. Many such young people have to think long and hard to come up with a friend of their acquaintance who does not or has not smoked dope.

The attitude of adults in this situation is often characterised by two polar opposite reactions.

Some accept children's drug-use as something that is now normal: 'We smoked weed when we were young – it's part of growing up!'

Others immediately look for someone to blame. This can either centre on the school or the home, especially when the drug-use of one's own child or pupil is experienced as a personal failing – unless of course one can find another, third party to take the blame.

Both attitudes preclude the possibility of really encountering the children and young people who are taking drugs, and divert attention from the real causes.

In relation to the phenomenon of addiction and drugs the concept of guilt or blame does not help us. Experience shows that children and young people from all classes and families, even the most caring and loving, turn to drugs. One must always take account of many different interrelating factors.

Where are the causes of drug-use to be found?
In the many conversations where young people have allowed me a glimpse into their souls – for which I am always genuinely grateful – the following motives for drug-use are the ones most frequently cited:

Fear – of the demands of a society based on achievement, of conflicts and confrontations
Lack – of love, protection, recognition
Longing – for warmth, light, harmony, intimacy,
for adventure, kicks, exhilaration,
for friends, belonging,
for calm and peace,
for meaning.

It is clear from what they tell me that we can no longer make do with simple answers to the question of why people take drugs. The motives are as individual as the drug-users themselves, and understandable as soon as one opens oneself to their inner soul state. Yet answers about the cause of drug-use are not only to be found in relation to each individual user's life-situation, but also, above all, by considering today's society.

Drug problems can no longer be ignored – they belong to our times.

> There is strength in understanding – the power of understanding is part of the process of healing.

Seeking the self

Over the course of the past century, as we have seen, social forms have increasingly dissolved. Even the nuclear family barely remains a sustaining force beyond childhood. Social communities, traditions and old norms collapse. Each individual must create his own network of relationships himself – a situation of freedom which humanity has never before experienced.

At the same time this situation represents an enormous challenge; for as norms and sustaining social forms fade, so a sense of inner void and loneliness increases – a situation which many try to escape through dependency on other people, particular kinds of experience or specific substances.

If the search for one's own identity ends here – in other words, if we do not become self-determining but remain under the sway of external influences – then this is an addiction phenomenon. This gives rise to a vicious circle of longing for more and more 'experiences', together with disappointment at the fact that we experience what we long for less and less.

Nowadays we are not only marked by an increasing outer lack of relatedness, a gulf between people and lack of social cohesion, but we are also in danger of an increasing lack of relationship with ourselves.

Thus we experience large gaps in the sense of our own health, in our relationship with our body and its needs, with time itself. We lose a healthy, loving, patient contact with ourselves and therefore also with our children.

What are human beings?

Safety, protection.
Then, a light; harsh, stabbing:
Cold walls, crying. I, a human being, am here.

Machine of flesh and blood –
Life made of motion, sense of time and feeling.
Miracle of more than nature,
Polluting nature, link in the chain of the masses,
Unit of group coercion
In search of the ego.

Live your I and you'll be free.
Love your world, and you will be born
Into the circling whirlpool of love,
For love is life.
Shout out your longing, cry hot
Tears and you'll be free.

Kristina, 16-years-old

> Only when we understand our children's sufferings can we give them what they need for healthy development.

Alienation today

The characteristics of our age make it clear how far the circumstances and conditions have changed in which our children are now growing up. The things that are no longer a matter of course for us adults and educators are not available, either, in the education our children assimilate.

We can only offer meaningful education and effective

prevention when we dedicate ourselves to our children's complex problems, without wringing our hands in despair, chafing at destiny or complaining mournfully about the state of modern culture. Our children inhabit particular conditions and times, and we need to get to proper grips with these.

I would therefore like to outline four characteristic types of alienation which all of us suffer, our children in particular.

Loss of relationship with one's own body

More and more frequently we have before us children who make it clear there is something screaming to get out of their body. One can have the sense that our children are stuck inside uncomfortable sheaths and wraps. The child experiences the body as a narrow, confining cell. He feels ill at ease because he

- has not slept enough
- does not move enough
- is poorly nourished
- wears clothes made of unpleasant materials
- has watched too much TV
- experiences an atmosphere of uncertainty (dispute, unhappiness)

When we plug young children in from an early age to the electronic 'grandmother' of TV or computer, we switch them off from ourselves and their experience of the world at the same time.

And adults expect such a child to behave well, be 'good', instead of seeing that he cannot possibly feel comfortable in his body.

We may, for instance, observe that a child has cold hands and feet, or that his skin suffers from poor circulation. If the body grows too cool/cold because of lacking physical or social 'skins', and becomes insensitive, it can no longer serve as a healthy instrument for the soul to express itself. As a result children become restless, nervous and aggressive.

In this context we also have to ask how far we are going to allow electronic media, such as TV or computer, to intrude into children's bedrooms. These create an artificial world full of illusions and condemn the viewer to total passivity.

But children are natural movers, and hindering their movement and activity has a paralysing effect, alienating them from their own intrinsic needs. Their movement is hampered when, for instance:

- they are driven about in a car more than they are allowed to move under their own steam;
- they are 'relieved' of the effort to stand upright and walk by means of a baby walker;
- they are prevented from experiencing the real world with all their senses but offered instead an illusory world through the TV screen, computer or game-boy display;
- they do not come into contact with the natural elements of earth, water, air and fire because there is no place or opportunity to experience these;
- they are prevented from 'sweating their way through' childhood illnesses, which they emerge from with greater strength and health.

> Children without a relationship to their own physical body and spatial environment experience a kind of homelessness and loss of trust in the world.

Loss of relationship to time and rhythm
A second type of alienation occurs where there is disregard for the rhythms of life. For instance, people bringing up children are less

and less aware of the importance of a daily rhythm in child development.

In many families there are no longer even shared mealtimes. Fast-food and the microwave menu are more and more the norm. A shared meal, perhaps with a grace beforehand, and not starting until everyone has been served, are regarded as old-fashioned – but they offer an important moment of pause and gathering in the day's flow, which might be worth considering.

It is rare in our hectic daily lives for people to cultivate a sense for the qualities of morning and evening, for them to start and finish the day together with their children: instead there are constant deadlines, things to be done, which turn each day into a uniform rush rather than a rhythm.

Likewise there is less and less awareness of the rhythm of the year, of the seasons and their festivals. The Christmas shop-window displays as early as September, and the chocolate bunnies in February are just one symptom of this.

Fewer and fewer children experience the rhythmic quality involved in the preparation, celebration and then ebbing of a festival. Ceremonies and rituals, where parents take time to experience structured sequences of time with reverence, patience and in leisure, in which children can feel sustained and enclosed, are increasingly vanishing from people's daily lives.

Rhythm gives children security and direction, and enhances their physical development. Children love repetition. If the child's daily life is rhythmically structured, so that for instance every morning begins with the same ritual, followed by a rhythmically ordered morning at nursery or school, and then an equally rhythmic afternoon at home,[1] the child's body and soul learn to breathe within these rhythms. Experiencing the rhythms of nature also belongs here.

> Children with no relationship to time and rhythm lose their trust and confidence in life and thus experience inner uncertainty.

Loss of relationship to soul forces

A third, common form of alienation is one which children experience in relation to their own soul forces and the soul forces of people in their environment. Time-consuming TV exposure reduces the time available to them to engage in friendships, with the conflict and conflict-resolution these involve. A cooling of the soul occurs: instead of encountering or conquering the world, it is all done for them as passive viewers of occurrences which they really wish to experience for themselves. If they do not experience sustaining and demanding soul relationships, the results of this 'cooling' process appear in adolescence at the latest. How much at risk young people can be when they have failed to develop a sense of themselves through real friendships can be seen from a survey in the USA of people under 18 who wished to attempt suicide but did not go through with it – half a million each year! They were asked what held them back from the attempt, and in most cases they replied that it was remembering a person with whom they felt a deep affinity or relationship.

> If real human relationships are no longer available, soul development comes to a halt.

Lack of commitment, relativism, indifference and even complete lack of interest in life are often the result. A computer firm's adverts can highlight this trend:

A spotlight beams in on adolescents who are quarrelling and seem unable to resolve the conflict. From the other side the suggestive image of a computer screen floats up, at which a happy, internet-surfing girl is busy chatting on-line to 'virtual' friends. A voice in the background warbles suggestively: 'No more conflicts – choose your friends yourself!'

Loss of relationship with oneself

The fourth type of alienation follows from the other three I have outlined: if trust in the environment, in the rhythms of life, in soul relationships with other people, is disturbed, we are unable to build up a healthy relationship with ourselves.

> When we lose touch with ourselves we become easy prey to manipulation and control by outside forces.

Children and adolescents experience this divorce from ideals and real, meaningful encounters with other people particularly because they see very few examples of a spiritual view of life in adults around them.

To sum up, we can observe that these types of loss of relationship devour the forces which children need to grow and develop in a healthy way. What are these forces of childhood?

The forces of childhood

A child is naturally endowed with trusting forces of *devotion*. In all helplessness he can entrust himself unconditionally to his environment.

These forces of devotion also allow children to *forgive* in a way that leaves us miles behind and shamefaced.

We can never again capture that state in which a playing child so completely gives himself up to an activity, *forgetting time and place*.

By nature children are *truthful,* as long as their development has not been disturbed, for they are still wholly one with themselves and the world.

These forces are under very serious threat in society, largely as a result of alienation of various kinds.

If childhood forces, these 'protecting relationship skins' are destroyed in early childhood, this has consequences for the rest of a person's life.

> People often try to use drugs to gain what was never fully experienced in childhood: trust in life, in the rhythms of time, in fellow human beings; the warmth of relationships and joy in existence.

Why Huckleberry Finn didn't get hooked

This is the title of a book by Eckhard Schiffer,[2] in which he describes addiction as follows:

Addiction has many faces and many causes. Addiction involves actions intended to alter a state of inner unhappiness, tension and restlessness or tormenting emptiness. In other words, lack of peace. So the aim is to attain gratification or fulfilment. Yet this path leads, via short-term illusory peace, to self-destruction. And people usually follow this path despite knowing the consequences and being 'well-informed'.

Schiffer asks: 'What has all this to do with Huckleberry Finn?' And he replies:

In Mark Twain's stories of Tom Sawyer, Huckleberry Finn is an affront to good, middle-class folks – lazy, unkempt, his father a violent man and heavy drinker, no mention even of a mother. Our modern ideas would lead us to think Huckleberry Finn must be a youngster at severe risk. Yet clearly Huck makes good...What's important is the sense of things the rascal Huck gives us in his rebellious-cum-creative thinking and actions... the inner feelings roused in us when we read what Huck says about his life: sympathy, laughter, nostalgia.

Huck embodies our usually suppressed longing for a world without certain norms, rules and laws, the adherence to which can make us ill; a world not pre-packaged in advance but experienced through all the senses, so that it becomes an adventure despite its apparent banality, and invites us to be adventurous in imagination.

What Huckleberry Finn has, despite the worst possible childhood conditions, is: time, imagination, a natural environment and a friend. He swims, dives, rows, climbs, carves wood, makes fires, fights, runs and leaps. He experiences the world with all his senses and completely as his needs dictate. He goes out to meet the world in the way he wants, without having anything forced on him that he does not like.

Even the difficult things he experiences are unable to rob him of his irrepressible joy in life. He keeps the reins of his life amidst a narrow-minded, middle-class society of fixed expectations. Untroubled and recalcitrant he follows the lead only of his imagination, his needs, his ideas. Addictive substances mean nothing to him – his life is far too lovely for him to want to sneak off from it.

1   In Germany and many other countries, young children only spend the morning at school rather than the whole day, as happens in England from the age of 5.
2   Eckhard Schiffer: *Warum Huckleberry Finn nicht süchtig wurde*, Weinheim 1999.

Addiction in all its various forms is avoidable if our children's world can be protected from destruction, and they can unfold their creative powers there.

E. Schiffer

6

Is prevention possible?

Our children's education is the subject of increasing concern and growing criticism. The very titles of books that have gained wide readership in the last few years point to a need to reflect on what our children need in order to mature into life-affirming adults.

'Yesterday's education, today's students, tomorrow's schools' by Peter Struck,[1] 'The End of Education' and 'The Disappearance of Childhood' by Neil Postman, 'Anxious, unhappy and restless children' by Henning Kohler', and 'Education in apocalyptic times' by Albert Schmelzer – all these are eloquent confirmation of the fact that it really is high time to develop fundamentally new ideas about education.

The environment our children inhabit has altered drastically in the last few years. Nevertheless children's basic needs are the same as they always were:

They wish to
- feel safe and protected
- be truly perceived
- work hard and do well
- learn
- understand the world and make it their own
- be loved

They need
- times of loving encounter in the family and at school
- space and opportunity for natural movement
- time to play imaginatively, so that time opens into timelessness

Sustaining the forces of childhood

Parents increasingly complain that their children no longer know how to play properly, have no imagination and find it difficult to concentrate on anything, do not trust easily, can no longer endure parents' tenderness, do not sleep enough and are nervous and lacking in respect.

Isn't this due to the fact that our children are rarely given the time and space to develop their childhood forces?
- When educational 'achievement' is the main, one-sided focus,
- when a child's development is judged according to fixed norms,
- when society's demands determine the course of education,
- when computer skills have to be learned in infancy,
- when children are turned into mini-adults,
- then the forces of childhood get lost; then childhood vanishes, and with it our future.

Prevention is all
that forms the will,
that strengthens the will,
that develops emotional and social capacities,
that develops power of judgement,
that enables us to distinguish between reality and illusion.

It is not by chance that this is happening in our times, which are marked by uncertainty and existential crisis. We all experience the collapsing social fabric, and the loneliness that is part of our new-won freedom. This is freedom that many people are afraid of, which they try to protect themselves from through high achievement, abiding by norms, controlling their image. Faced by this challenge, many people flee into the illusory world of an addiction. The uncomfortable path of freedom is exchanged for the apparently easier path of dependency – a particularly ominous symptom of our time, given that the WHO predicts that in a few decades every second person in the world will be a drug addict.

It is hardly surprising that our children most clearly embody the consequences of such anxieties.

Prevention today

How can we educate our children so that they are equal to this world, so that they can develop the necessary strength to take hold of the world as it is and realise their impulses for the future?

Is preventive education a possibility? Prevention certainly cannot mean that we prevent them from encountering drugs or other addictive substances. Instead we need to try to strengthen our children and adolescents so that they do not succumb when addiction rears its head.

> Trust and reliability experienced in childhood form a sustaining foundation in adolescence when all outer supports and bridges collapse.

Creating trust
Frequently children with drugs problems have no inner contact with their parents any longer. Parents and children may still live under one roof, but no conversations take place. There is no exchange and expression of feelings, experiences and thoughts.

That is why it is so enormously important to cultivate contact and conversation at an age when children themselves still seek closeness and attention from their parents. If warmth lives between parents and child, an indestructible inner relationship of trust develops, which continues to sustain the adolescent when she outwardly separates from her parents. This inner contact to people she formerly trusted so deeply often becomes the saving grace at a time when all old relationships break down.

It is therefore important during the early years to give the child a special time at least once a day when she knows: Now my parents are wholly there for me, nothing can take this time away, the telephone will not ring and no one can come barging in and take my parents' attention away from me.

> Preventive education has succeeded when the adolescent can distinguish between illusion and reality.

Ending the day in calm and peace

Children experience their little conflicts and annoyances, their unhappiness with their friends, brothers and sisters, and parents. It is a blessing for every child if she learns to make peace in the evening with the upsets of the day. It is very good for the child to experience the loving attention of her parents in this free space lifted out of the ordinary run of things. In this atmosphere of soul warmth it is possible to look back on both the good and not so good events of the day, to feel embraced and enclosed in love and warmth, feel truly 'held'.

Children who are accompanied from the day to the night in this way can fall asleep peacefully and wake up refreshed in the morning.

This evening dialogue – which needs regularity rather than a lot of time – is irreplaceable, for through it the child experiences a loving perception of her individual being, which gives her an inner sense of herself. Once mother and/or father have recognized the fundamental importance of this, they will find or make the time to provide these precious minutes in the evening, whether they are both involved in child-care or are single parents.

What I myself experience is more than any drug can offer

Sense experiences in the first few years of life are the best instructors, enabling us to relate to the world via physical body, soul experience and spiritual encounter in a way that gives us a sense of ourselves as creative agent rather than victim of circumstances. Experiencing the body in a healthy way develops a secure sense of our own self-worth, as well as a sense of our own activity and accompanying sense of life: the world and the way it is formed depends on me, rather than the other way round.

Thus stimulation, schooling and care of the senses are the best means of prevention.

Rudolf Steiner never tired of pointing out how decisive care of the senses is as a basis for a person's development and the free unfolding of her personality and ego.

In her book 'Children at the doctor's surgery'[2] Michaela Glöckler has given a very clear overview of the twelvefold nature of sense experience, basing this on Rudolf Steiner's comprehensive teaching about the senses. This adds to the generally recognized senses the further senses of life, word or language, thought and ego which he researched and described.

In the first seven-year period the body develops self-perception chiefly through the senses of touch, life, movement and balance.

> **The sense of touch**
> mediates
> self-awareness at the body's periphery via touch.
> Security through physical contact. Confidence in life.

Ways of nurturing it
- alternating between being alone and being safe and secure; between delicate physical contact and being left alone, in peace; being able to let go is just as important as embracing.

Harmful influences
- external care without inner acceptance of the child
- too much protecting or leaving alone
- touching that gratifies oneself rather than expressing love for the child

> **The sense of life**
> mediates
> comfort, experience of harmony, sense of the interrelatedness of things.

Ways of nurturing it
- rhythmic structure to the day
- confident outlook on life
- experiencing 'good measure' and timing, i.e. of arrangements that harmonise
- pleasure at mealtimes

Harmful influences
- argument, violence, anxiety
- hectic rush, fright
- unhappiness
- extremes, excess

- nervousness
- lack of interrelationship between things that occur

The sense of movement

mediates

perception of one's own movement, sense of freedom and
sense of self-control through control of one's movements

Ways of nurturing it
- allow children to be active
- arrange a child's bedroom so that everything is within reach and
free play is possible
- purposeful movement sequences

Harmful influences
- continually impose particular prohibitions on children
- lack of stimulus to activity through passivity or failure to offer
good examples/models
- couch potato habits in front of the TV
- playing with automatic toys that make children mere watchers

---

The sense of balance

mediates

a sense of balance, equilibrium, moments of calm, self-confidence.

Ways of nurturing it
- movement games, see-saw, stilts, jumping etc.
- calmness and certainty when relating to children
- striving for inner balance by the adult

Harmful influences
- poverty of movement
- inner agitation

- depression, resignation
- weariness with life
- restlessness
- inner conflict

Particularly in the second phase of childhood, when the child begins school, a more refined perception of the external world arises, coupled with very sensitive self-awareness. These perceptions depend especially on the senses of smell, taste, sight and warmth.

The sense of smell
mediates
a link with what emanates smell or fragrance

Ways of nurturing it
- Seeking differentiated experiences of smell or fragrance from plants, foods, in the town, country etc

Harmful influences
- badly-aired rooms
- unpleasant smells or odours
- impressions and modes of behaviour that arouse disgust

The sense of taste
mediates sweet, sour, salt, bitter;
together with smell it gives rise to differentiated taste

Ways of nurturing it
- accentuating the intrinsic taste of foods through the way they are cooked
- 'tasteful' judgment of people and things
- forming surroundings in an aesthetic way

Harmful influences
- tendencies to uniformity of taste (e.g. 'ketchup on everything')
- tasteless remarks
- lack of tact
- unaesthetic surroundings

The sense of sight
mediates light and colour

Ways of nurturing it
- drawing attention to fine colour distinctions in nature through one's own interest in this
- harmonious colour combinations in dress and home décor

Harmful influences
- over-rigidity through destructive or 'blatant' images
- harsh colours
- too much TV
- gloomy mood
- apathy
- colourless, dreary surroundings

The sense of warmth
mediates experiences of warmth and cold

Ways of nurturing it
- nurturing the warmth organism through clothing appropriate for each age
- emanating soul and spiritual warmth

Harmful influences
- extreme measures to 'toughen up' children
- overheated rooms

- insufficient clothing
- cold, impersonal atmosphere
- exaggerated/untruthful 'warm-heartedness'

In the third phase of development, leading into adolescence, the young person becomes still more sensitive to the external world, at the same time structuring her inner world anew. In this phase, it is predominantly the senses of hearing, word, thought and ego which develop.

> **The sense of hearing**
> mediates experiences of tone.
> Opening of the inner soul space.

Ways of nurturing it
- when reading and telling stories to children, adapt the speed of speaking to the children's capacity to take things in
- singing and making music

Harmful influences
- acoustic overload, especially through electronic media (too loud, too quick, not human or personal enough)
- superficial or dishonest speaking
- impersonal intonation and way of speaking

> **The sense of word**
> mediates the experience of form and physiognomy (sense of form)
> which extends to grasping the vocalised form of a word

Ways of nurturing it
- warm, warm-hearted intonation
- warm outward behaviour in gesture and body language
- harmonious relation of inner experience and outward expression

(for otherwise untrue impressions arise)
– having a sense for individual expression

Harmful influences
– disparaging gestures
– cool, neutral behaviour, so that children do not know whether parents are happy, sad, attentive or uninterested
– every form of lie, so that inner and outer experiences do not match

---

The sense of thought
mediates direct grasping of a thought context

Ways of nurturing it
– cultivating truthfulness and consistency
– interrelationship of things and processes to one another
– experiencing a meaningful context in one's surroundings

Harmful influences
– senseless actions
– confused, uncoordinated thinking
– distortions of meaning and purpose
– thought associations without sense

The sense of ego
mediates experience of another's being. Direct experience of the other's character and inner configuration

---

Ways of nurturing it
– early intimate experience of a loving relationship with a parent figure
– love of adults for each other and for the child
– cultivation of meeting and encounter

- truly perceiving the other (Martin Buber's 'You')

Harmful influences
- lack of interest, disregard and other forms of lovelessness
- media consumption and subjection to 'virtual realities', where no real meeting with another can take place
- materialistic ideas about the human being
- sexual abuse[3]

Of course, full and complete development of all the senses can only be a goal we strive for. But knowing about the cultivation of the senses and its importance for ego development does give us necessary guidelines for prevention that works. As we shall see later, one of the main criteria for successful therapy with drugs patients lies in developing senses which have been dormant previously.

1   *Erziehung von gestern, Schüler von heute, Schule von morgen*
2   Michaela Glöckler. Wolfgang Goebel: *Die Kindersprechstunde,* Stuttgart 1998
3   Ibid

It isn't a question of battling against *drugs,*
but of fighting for
the individual who has to overcome them

Tenet of drugs therapy

7

What can I do, when…?

A non-dialogue

- You're ruining your health with that stuff!
- So? And is your rush and hurry, your drinking and smoking any better?
- You're living in a fantasy world of drugs!
- Is your world of work any more real? Do you ever ask yourself what you're really doing?
- You're isolating yourself from everyone around you!
- And what do you care? Who do you think you're really living with? You don't even know who I am!
- Things can't carry on like this. What are you going to do with your life?
- No idea, but at least I'll have more fun than you!

Whether spoken or unspoken, this non-dialogue carries on endlessly between the generations.

Do we really hear the longing expressed in it for a full and fulfilling life? Can we bear to hear the accusation that our own lives are hardly exemplary?

In November 99 the *Süddeutsche Zeitung* reported on the first distance learning school for school refusers:

- approximately 70,000 children and young people refuse to attend school in Germany;[1]
- in some cities there are extreme cases where up to a third of pupils stay away from school, absolutely refusing to attend over months or even years.[2]

> Children no longer find the stability in their families which they need. They turn to their schools to find it, but schools have largely become mere 'achievement zones'.[3]

Drugs as avoidance

If our children and adolescents are fleeing from reality in such enormous numbers, our first task is to face this fact with a fair and open mind.

Regarding drug-use as the work of the devil, and simply rejecting it, does not begin to do justice to this contemporary phenomenon. Panic – so often the stock response whenever drug-use is discovered – does not help us either.

Approving of drug-use, on the other hand, because of its likely effects, is also far too one-sided:

- The spiritual experiences induced by drugs are actually not purely spiritual, since they are dependent on the drug and thus necessarily arise through a toxic effect on the body.
- Positive changes in the life of a former drug-user who has overcome his habit are not an argument for drug-use. How do we know, beforehand, that he will actually manage to give up? Thousands of addicts tell us a different story.

We must try to show adolescents that they cannot always be clear about unconscious soul processes, nor direct and manage them as they intend.

'I'm in control of it' is one of the most commonly cited arguments of 'dope-heads'. But that is exactly what no adolescent can guarantee, even when he's just starting out on drug-use. Taking the drug in the first place depends on his will, but the subsequent effect is dictated solely by the substance itself; and that is not subject to self-control.

> Addiction is always a craving that has come to rest in its object and goal. Therefore an antidote to the fixed state of addiction is movement – physical movement, emotional/mental movement, spiritual movement.

What is very important nowadays is the loving – and not panic-raising – observation of teachers and parents: am I aware

* under what circumstances drugs are being taken?
* whether experimentation with drugs is going on?
* whether drug-use is a kind of self-medication (as with Benjamin, see page 12)
* whether there is an existential crisis playing into drug-use?
* whether deep changes are apparent?

Aspects of criminality, of legality or illegality are completely irrelevant here. What is needed, instead, is the loving, therapeutic stance and the will to help an individual develop.

Adolescents are asking us to change our attitudes. It is not a question of battling *against* drugs, but of fighting *for* something – *for ego activity, for the conditions necessary to the ego's full unfolding.*

If this battle for the development of ego activity in children and adolescents succeeds, then they all have a chance to counteract the temptations of drugs.

The basic gesture of every drug-use, as of every other form of addiction (such as the urge to criticise, work-addiction and many other everyday dependencies) is that of fixity and rigidity. All addiction prevention, and also the overcoming of every dependency, must therefore necessarily involve striving for movement.

> What we need today is not so much drugs education, not norms of achievement and career paths determined by others, but chances to learn – in which we learn to endure defeat, failure and crises, and come to understand and inwardly overcome them.
>
> Secondary pupil, Year 12

The simplest thing, certainly, is to offer movement in the physical realm.

But what about the soul? What are we offering our children and adolescents in the emotional realm? Do they experience

- that we feel good about our lives,
- that work can also be pleasurable and not only tedious,
- that there are important, purposeful things to be done,
- that we keep trying afresh, with new hope,
- that conflicts and crises are a difficult but worthwhile challenge, which we use to develop,
- that mistakes and failings are important learning opportunities to try again, to do better next time,
- that we are not only interested in the good but also in evil, because it has a necessary task in our time,
- that we love the time we live in, just as it is?

What can I do at home when…?

Based on her wide experience, Else Meier – one of the most impressive individuals in the field of drugs issues – has drawn up ten rules for parents to help them deal with an advanced stage of drug-use by their children. These rules are so apt and helpful that I would like to cite them here:

1 Free yourself from the idea that you can compel the addict to see the error of his ways. He is living in a different reality, his own.

2 Therefore oppose your reality to his as calmly and surely as possible. 'That's the way you see things, but we see and feel things differently.'

3 Don't waste any time looking for indications and traces of possible drug-use.

4 Get the whole family to practise unified and consistent behaviour in this regard, and don't try to justify this behaviour to the addict.

5 Do not do the slightest thing for the addict which he is capable of doing for himself.

6 Instead, give more time to your own interests and those of the rest of the family. This will give the addict a painful awareness of how much the drug is isolating him.

7 In his presence speak about your experiences, understanding, feelings, about joys but also difficulties. If not with him, then at least when he is present. He hears more than he acknowledges.

8 Counteract his consumption of artificial experiences with your own real experience, oppose his drug-based communication with a true sense of togetherness, rather than discussing it in theory.

9 Don't allow your thoughts to be stuck in the past or fly off into the future, but have new courage for each day that comes.

10 Keep your patience, practise composure and do not lose hope.

These rules help parents clearly oppose the drugs world, which their child has entered, with their own distinct world, providing a clarity which can help show the drug-user the extent to which he has already fallen prey to the power and laws of the drug.

> What serves development is good – what hinders it bad.

What can I do at school when...?

Let me give a few answers to typical questions I encounter in schools.

Shouldn't every school draw up a clear list of rules which preclude harmful drug-use at school?

Fixed rules and judgements aiming to prevent pupils' drug-use will not be much help. This has been clearly shown in the past by official drugs policy. It cannot be a matter of 'preventing', 'isolating' and 'excluding', but chiefly of 'understanding'.

But of course there are rules which apply to every school: drug-use is not desirable. Drugs are not to be taken at school. And if this happens there will be consequences.

In addition each school should adhere to the principle that no dealing is to take place on school grounds. If this happens action must be taken immediately and the dealer removed from the social context. Thus there is a fundamental rule which applies to everyone: drug-use is not regarded as the norm. If it occurs it must be dealt with in a way that takes account of the individual pupil and his situation, and this in turn requires flexibility.

Even experimenting with drugs can be of benefit to a person's development. Of course we cannot generalise, for *no one can know beforehand* whether a drug experience will lead to inner rigidity, to the gesture of addiction, or instead to a broadening of horizons and further personal development.

So you wouldn't simply recommend that teachers ought not to countenance drugs?!

It is no use us telling young people not to try drugs. Adolescents have a natural desire to expand their consciousness in this way.

At puberty adolescents feel themselves imprisoned in their bodies, subjected to rules, constricted by models of behaviour, and they cannot simply take all these things on board and live with them uncritically. There is a revolutionary, explosive power in every adolescent seeking to burst these same constrictions and limits, and to reach out far beyond all given boundaries. Thus drugs have a very natural affinity with adolescence, for it is only through the greatest inner efforts that young people can break through to joyful and liberating spiritual experiences. But nowadays our young people no longer have sufficient models and examples, people from whom they might learn how to overcome conflicts and how to endure bad patches.

> The drug holds out the promise of what we do not achieve in the social sphere!
>
> If human encounter offers no inner warmth, we will not be able to hinder the illusory warmth offered by drugs.

As long as we only make demands of the other, in human encounter as well as at critical moments of our lives, rather than making equal demands on ourselves; and as long as we behave unsocially and do not support and acknowledge each other's development, we should not be surprised that drugs are nowadays so attractive and becoming more so all the time. We cannot do battle with the one without doing something for the other – it doesn't add up.

I would never tell adolescents to go ahead and try drugs. But *if* they do, we should not panic immediately; and above all we shouldn't exclude them straight away from the school setting.

Instead we should very carefully examine the underlying motives and the drug-user's individual capacities: how can we compensate here? How can we help to counterbalance this through what we do at school? When is a specific course of therapy necessary? When must we look outside school for help?

Are lessons the right place, anyway, to confront the drugs problem?

Yes, definitely! Where else will children and adolescents get clear, objective information? For objective information is the very first step. Not panic, not fear, but clarity is needed about the whole sphere of drugs and their effects.

Whenever I work with secondary pupils and quite soberly describe the facts of Ecstasy's effects – such as its attack on the brain's synaptic realm, the irreversible processes it calls forth, the release of the whole serotonin content causing the desired euphoria, resulting biochemical processes due to this stress situation in the synapse realm, the possible endogenous depressions that follow – then, to my consternation, I often find that pupils only ask one further question: Why has no one ever told us this before?

In that case, aren't a few lessons enough to deal with the theme of drugs?

No, a few lessons are not enough. It is a fundamental characteristic of drugs that they lurk underground, in concealment. This is partly because every drug-use is treated as something bad, morally wrong, something to be kept hidden, which cannot be openly discussed but only spoken of via rumour and suspicion. This concealment clings to drugs as a diabolical side effect, one can say. The first thing to do is break through this dark and hidden region which shrouds drug-use.

> Where openness, clarification, objective criteria for judgement hold sway, drugs are demystified and their power is taken from them.

For teachers and parents this involves:

- getting to know the facts – as far as both drugs and also drug-users are concerned;
- overcoming all condemnation, and learning to perceive and understand phenomena objectively;
- ridding themselves of their fear of drug-use, and focusing their perceptions and efforts on the drug-user, rather than on the drug;
- making sure they do not exclude and vilify but work lovingly towards reintegration.

For pupils this involves:

- having trust in their teachers
- speaking openly about their problems, or about how they see others' problems
- facing themselves critically, with responsibility, freedom and initiative.

If the way drugs work is clearly communicated, if open conversation can be held about people's very different individual reactions to substances, and their unpredictability, the drug will largely lose the allure of something hidden and forbidden.

It will be clear from this that we are not talking about a lesson or two on drugs, but about a process which all must be prepared to enter into. How useful such a process is, despite all the associated obstacles and difficulties, often only becomes apparent in retrospect.

1   The figures for England are a similar percentage of the total school population
2   Cited by Jutta Pilgram in the *Süddeutsche Zeitung*
3   Else Meyer: *Eltern im Drogenproblem. Erfahrungen durch Selbsthilfe,* St. Augustin 1993

The educative principle becomes
the principle of therapy…

8

Anthroposophical drug therapy

Stages of therapy

Anthroposophical therapy centres have developed approaches to healing out of the awareness that many addicts suffer from a lack of warmth and a deep, purposeful sense of life.

In the first stages of therapy our task is to replace the passive and illusory experiences which addiction offers, with true, reality-imbued experiences. The various steps and stages of therapy arise from an insight into the fact that the addict craves the kinds of experience normally undergone in the first three seven-year periods of life.

To clarify the aims of such therapy I would first like to describe phases of normal, undisturbed development up to the age of 22.

Developmental stages of the first three seven-year periods

Basis of an individual's healthy development in the *first seven-year period* is a full, vital encounter with one's own physical body.

Sense activity, orientated mainly towards the body, needs to be cultivated and nurtured by offering the child, with her innate urge to imitate, sufficient healthy and real models. Purposeful activity in the child's presence, as well as a rhythmic sequence to the day, have special importance at this period. These work right in to the very structure of organs and bodily functions. This enables the child's will to develop in a healthy way.

> The *second seven-year period* is the phase where vital feelings develop. The examples adults give have a decisive role to play here.

At this stage it is important for the child to learn to take her lead from the structured feeling life of adults, as well as being encouraged to enliven the senses which connect her with the outer world. At this age children need an ordered and beautifully formed environment. The world must become a field of experience that holds great interest and promise. During this period it is of decisive import- ance for the child to be able to link herself with her surroundings in a feeling way, and to feel accepted and loved. Only then can she find her bearings and develop a healthy life of feeling.

> In the *third seven-year period* an adolescent needs a vital involve- ment with the mind and spirit. Her intense encounter and confrontation with the world of the senses must find its bearings through ideals, and love of truth and reality.

A young person needs to have a deep experience of the difference between truth and error, reality and illusion. This also involves giving adolescents increasing responsibility, so that they can gain their own experiences of the surrounding world. They must be allowed to make mistakes. But this is also just the time when they need the world and other people to offer them stimulus, example and experience. Enthusiasm and engagement have a wakening effect on their mental and spiritual capacities, while resignation and negativity have a paralysing effect. This is a time when adults especially need to demonstrate that they can continually renew themselves and start afresh, thus offering the adolescent scope for his developing 'social and understanding senses', as Rudolf Steiner also calls them.

So we can see how the human ego develops in the first three seven-year periods: in physical activity, soul activity and thinking activity. While we are still developing through, and fully immersed in, these realms of activity, we are not yet able to confront the world as free, self-determining individuals. This is only possible when these forms of activity come to an initial conclusion between the ages of 18 and 21.

Every *premature* confrontation with contemporary phenomena deprives a young person's ego activity of forces which it needs. This can mean that ego strength is weakened, and less available in later life for genuine encounter with the external world, for dealing with the attacks it mounts on the individual.

The stages of addiction therapy try to enable the patient to catch up on the experiences of these three seven-year periods, in such a way that she can offset the gaps in her experience which, at least partly, led her into addiction.

The therapeutic journey

For years now, anthroposophical therapy centres have been working to achieve this. The therapeutic path, which can basically be divided into four stages, shows how therapists undertake this in community with the patients:

- At stage 1 the therapist needs to attend to her patient with warm interest, asking the inner question: 'Who are you?' The aim here is to understand the patient as deeply as possible, both in her inner being and her difficulties.

- At stage 2 the therapist connects with the patient, perceiving her fully and devotedly in order to accompany her through the stages of healing, and as far as possible put aside her (the therapist's) own personal wishes. This means that the therapist frees herself from her own ideas about what the patient is like and how she ought to be, striving only to perceive the actual reality, with love for the smallest detail.

- At stage 3 the therapist needs to accompany the patient through the crises necessary for her healing. It cannot be a matter of a quick cure, of merely encouraging sympathy or offering understanding and comfort. The patient has to go through the depths of her crisis alone if it is really to help her undergo inner transformation. The only real help in this process is for the patient to have a loving companion beside her. At this stage the therapist holds painful, probing conversations with the patient about her biography, seeking a cause for her avoidance and flight from life. The patient has to want to search actively and autonomously for her wholly individual life task. This striving for the guiding force in one's own life sets a counterbalance against the drug and its spiralling attack on the core of the individual.

  If the patient, through her own ego activity, comes closer to her life's purpose or sense through therapy, she will then be able to continue living at a level which is more fitting for her than was the life she fled by means of addiction.

> The battle with the 'demon' of addictive substances can only be won by a community which finds a source of spiritual strength to draw on.

If she can develop her ego strength sufficiently to reach this point, the patient must now carefully nurture it and counteract every temptation the moment it raises its head. If she allows this new awareness to be obscured even for a moment, there is grave danger of a relapse.

- **The fourth stage** demands extreme selflessness of the therapist, for she must loosen her connection with the patient as the latter develops increasing autonomy. Then the former addict can enter into a new connection with the world with newly won awareness, taking responsibility for herself.

For the addict this is a path of self-discovery, and for the therapist a path of selfless devotion to the patient. The therapist can only find the strength to undertake this by continually striving to overcome self-seeking desires and egotistic feelings. Each time she manages this she gains more strength for her task. On her own she would not have sufficient strength to confront herself and her failings or combat the demon of addictive substance. This battle cannot effectively be waged by one person alone, but by a community of people which finds a spiritual source of strength to draw on. In these therapeutic communities therefore, at regular intervals, members work together to research and deepen their understanding of addiction, by seeking the spiritual sources of knowledge or understanding they need.

*I am a free man! Under no circumstances do I wish to
be an average human being.
I have a right to be different if I can be.
I wish for opportunities not certainties,
I want to undergo risk, to long for something and realise it,
be shipwrecked and have success.
I have learned to act for myself, to look the world in the eye
and recognise what my task is, my work.
All this is what we mean when we say:
I am a free man.*

Albert Schweizer

9

I have a dream

What would be the best possible way of strengthening children and adolescents nowadays, so that they cope with an addictive society? They would need to develop:

- self-will: I will/want to do something and I can
- self-esteem: I am loved for who I am, my feelings have value
- capacity to converse: I can discuss problems and difficulties, I can communicate
- independence and responsibility for oneself: I can take the personal space I need and am learning to accept the consequences of my own actions
- conflict capacity: I am not thrown by every problem; conflicts are just the practice weights for my soul muscles. I can gain strength from them
- independent activity: when I engage myself and produce my own ideas, visions and suggestions, I am not a victim but the creator of my own circumstances
- capacity for experience: no drug can offer me what I myself experience
- joy in life: I can take pleasure each day in some small miracle on this earth, in human meetings, in natural phenomena, perhaps also in some little step forward I take in my own development.

These are ideals, the realisation of which is no doubt daunting to all of us. But success lies in small steps. The decisive thing is not to ask how children or adolescents can best attain these qualities, but rather how I can create the right conditions to enable the child or adolescent *himself* to want to develop them gradually.

Conclusion

If I had a particular wish in writing this book then it was to deepen people's understanding of addiction so that one thing, at least, would become apparent: the pain and difficulty endured by fellow human beings who are addicts.

Only by shifting our focus away from one-sided condemnations to a fuller image of the human being and his unquenched longings, will we be able to find ways of offering individual help.

Only when we become more open for the experiences of today's adolescent soul, with its burdens but also its purposes, motives and spiritual messages to us, can we gain perspectives which renew our capacity to meet and help the other.

So let us be touched, moved by their drug-use, their resignation, their gestures of flight!

Let's overcome our short-sighted complaining, as well as our mis-guided, indifferent 'tolerance' – both leave our adolescents equally in the lurch, without any clear guidance.

What they need nowadays, more than anything else, is something that even the highest of high-tech media cannot offer: a meeting with adults, soul to soul, unmasked, open and honest.

In the true encounter with an adult and his behaviour, through his personal engagement, dismay and consternation, adolescents can become aware of the boundaries they have overstepped.

In the shared struggle for boundaries that make sense, young people can learn to find their way anew and take responsibility for themselves and others.

These are steps towards adulthood which depend significantly on how we adults let ourselves in for open encounter, so that a living relationship becomes possible. Fixed and rigid programmes can only hinder this process; agreements worked out together with an adolescent, on the other hand, delineate the necessary boundaries that give each person the personal space he needs. What we need are individual solutions and clear consequences, as the vital precondition for a relaxed relationship between adults and adolescents: a relationship whose clarity allows room for humour even when the limits are overstepped.

Much of this book is only a fragmentary outline. The bibliography may stimulate readers to deepen their engagement with this theme.

I hope that what I have written will help people to find renewed pleasure in their encounters with fellow human beings, with adolescents, with the world, with themselves. Human encounter enriches us with aspects of the other we did not know before, broadening our understanding and continually deepening our experience of freedom and truth.

Your children are not your children.
They are the sons and daughters of Life's longing for itself.
They come through you but not from you,
And though they are with you yet they belong not to you.
You may give them your love but not your thoughts,
For they have their own thoughts.
You may house their bodies but not their souls,
For their souls dwell in the house of tomorrow,
which you cannot visit even in your dreams.
You may strive to be like them, but seek not to make them like you.
For life goes not backwards nor tarries with yesterday.
You are the bows from which your children as
living arrows are sent forth…
Let your bending in the Archer's hand be for gladness!

Kahlil Gibran

Bibliography

D. Bäuerle: *Suchtprävention und Drogenprävention in der Schule,* Munich 1996

A. Braun: *Weniger ist oft mehr,* Munich 1998

Bundeszentrale für gesundheitliche Aufklärung, 51101 Köln: *Kinder stark machen – zu stark für Drogen,* Munich 1998

K. Dohmen (ed.): *Drogen – eine Herausforderung für Schule und Gesellschaft,* Cologne 1993

B. Donaghy: *Anna's Story,* Angus and Robertson (Harper Collins Australia) 1996

R. Dunselman: *An Stelle des Ich – Rauschdrogen und ihre Wirkung,* Stuttgart 1996

F. Fredersdorf: *Leben ohne Drogen – Zwei Jahrzehnte Syanon,* Weinheim 1995

L. Hillenberg / B. Fries: *Starke Kinder – zu stark für Drogen.* Handbuch zur praktischen Suchtvorbeugung, Munich 1993

E. Hübner: *Drogen verstehen – Kinder lieben – Erziehung wagen,* Stuttgart 1996

M. Hülsmann: *Risse in der Seele,* Düsseldorf 1994 (biographical sketch)

K. Hurrelmann / U. Engel: *Was Jugendliche wagen. Eine Längsschnittstudie über Drogenkonsum, Stressreaktionen und Deliquenz im Jugendalter,* Weinheim 1998

K. Hurrelmann / H. Petermann: *Drogen, Konsum und Missbrauch im Jugendalter,* Neuwied 1999

Jahrbuch Sucht 1999. Ed.: *Deutsche Hauptstelle gegen Suchtgefahren,* Geesthacht 1998

Kollehn / Weber (eds.): *Der drogengefährdete Schüler,* Düsseldorf 1991

O. Koob: *Drogensprechstunde,* Stuttgart 1997

G. Kruse et al.: *Fix(en) und fertig? Drogen und Drogenhilfe in Deutschland,* Bonn 1996

P. Mann: *Hasch – Zerstörung einer Legende, Ffm. 1996* (especially for young people)

E. Meyer: *Eltern im Drogenproblem – Erfahrungen durch Selbsthilfe,* St. August 1993

A. Sahihi: *Designerdrogen,* Munich 1993

N. Saunders et al.: *Ecstasy,* Zürich 1994

E. Schiffer: *Warum Huckleberry Finn nicht süchtig wurde,* Weinheim / Berlin 1994

R. Schindler / S. Jucker: *Mia, was ist ein Trip?* Zürich/Kiel/Vienna 1994

W. Schmidbauer / J. vom Scheidt: *Handbuch der Rauschdrogen.* Ffm. 1998

J. Schmitt-Kilian: *Drogen,* Munich 1994

v. Soer / Stratenwerth: *Süchtig geboren,* Hamburg 1991

J. v. Soer / M. Wolny-Follath: *H wie Heroin – Betroffene erzählen ihr Leben,* Hamburg 1990

K.L. Täschner: *Drogen, Rausch und Sucht,* Stuttgart 1994

B. van Treeck: *Partydrogen,* Berlin 1997

F. Vogt: *Drogensucht – Weckruf unserer Zeit,* Bad Liebenzell 1998

F. Vogt: *In Ruhe wahrnehmen und abwägen. Interview über den pädagogischen Umgang mit Drogenfragen.* Special edition of the magazine Das Goetheanum, no.11, 15.3.1998

M. Vogt: *Sehn-Sucht,* Lausanne 1994

Further Reading

M. Gossop: *Living with Drugs.* Ashgate Publishing, Aldershot, 1996

Emma Fossey: *Growing Up with Alcohol.* Routledge 1999

Scottish Drugs Forum: *Drugfax: A guide for people who provide information about drugs.* ISBN 0-951976-11-7, 1997

M. Plant: *Risk Takers: Alcohol, Drugs, Sex and Youth.* Routledge 1992

A. Tayler: *Street Drugs: a guide to legal and illegal drugs in use today.* ISBN 0-340609-75-3, 1995

Gary Hayes (ed): *Drugs: Your Questions Answered.* A student reader. (2nd edition). ISBN 0-9458830-33-6, DrugScope, 2000

Matthew Collin: *The Story of Ecstasy Culture and Acid House.* ISBN 1-852423-77-3, 1997

Addresses

Helplines and advice centres in England:

Alcohol Concern
For information on local alcohol support services. Open Monday–
Friday 9:30am–5:30pm.
Tel: 020 7928 7377
www.alcoholconcern.org.uk

Cocaine Anonymous
Has meetings and a helpline for cocaine users.
Tel: 020 7284 1123

Drug info website: www.drugworld.org

Drugs in Schools Helpline
Helpline for those who have concerns about drug related issues
within schools. Open Monday–Friday 10:00am–5:00pm.
Tel: 0845 738 6666

National drugs helpline (for help with all kinds of drug-related
issues): 0800 776600

Telephone counselling for addiction troubles or for those affected by others' drug use.
Frank O'Hare, Dip. Addiction, 0141 400 6456

Life Education Centres, organisation for drug prevention education.
1st Floor, 53-56 Great Sutton Street, London EC1 0DG.
Tel: 020 7490 3210 Fax: 020 7490 3610

General information:

ADFAM National
Runs the National Telephone Helpline for the Families and Friends of Drug Users. Provides confidential support and information. Open Monday–Friday 10:00am–5:00pm and Tuesday 10:00am–7:00pm.
Waterbridge House, 32-36 Loman Street, London SE1 0EE.
Tel: 020 7928 8900

Drugscope
32-36 Loman Street, London SE1 0EE.
Tel: 020 7928 1211
www.drugscope.org.uk

Each county in England has a **Drug (and Alcohol) Action Team Co-ordinator** (DAT), who is located at the Health Authority and should have all the local information on support and agencies dealing with Drug issues.

Your local drugs project (harm reduction policy) may offer a range of services including needle exchange/counselling/information and other support for addicts and those with concerns around drugs

Information on Rehabilitation:

Addaction

Helping individuals and communities to manage the effects of drug and alcohol misuse.
Addaction Central Office, 67–69 Cowcross Street
London EC1M 6PU
Tel: 020 7251 5860 Fax: 020 7251 5890
www.addaction.org.uk

European Association for the Treatment of Addiction (EATA)
32–36 Loman Street, London SE1 0EE
www.eata.org.uk

Magazine:

Addiction Today
122A Wilton Road, London SW1V 1JZ
Tel: 020 7233 5333
www.addictiontoday.co.uk

Self help:

Alcoholics Anonymous (AA)
Tel: 020 7833 0022

Narcotics Anonymous (NA)
Tel: 020 7251 4007

Overeaters Anonymous
Tel: 07000 784985

Inishfree

Inishfree is a new initiative (working out of Anthroposophy) which is in the process of trying to set up a rural community in Gloucestershire for people who are overcoming alcohol and/or drug addiction aged 18+.

It is aiming to provide training and skills in a farming environment as well as therapeutic support such as massage, Eurythmy (movement therapy), artistic therapies, biographical work and counselling.

Work would be created on a farm/small holding that needs a lot of attention, bringing life and substance back into the land itself and the larger community.

Training will include
- building/renovating, painting and decorating
- running the household, cooking, baking and catering
- growing vegetables and establishing a market garden (organic/biodynamic)

In the future keeping livestock, such as sheep, goats, chickens as well as working with horses will be a fundamental part of the recovery process.

Various **craft workshops** will be offered as needed and as facilities allow. We hope to complement the work and therapies with a rich **cultural life**, which will also contribute to the life of the local community.

In order to achieve sustainability we will sell some of our produce and offer various services to the wider community: recycling and environmental projects for example.

At the moment we are offering support for parents, partners, friends and carers of those suffering from addiction over the phone as well as face to face. Please use the number below if you think we might be able to help you.

We are looking for co-workers with a passion for working in any of the above fields as well as wanting to work with people who are trying to rediscover their potential. We hope to be set up by the end of 2002.

For more information please write to
Inishfree, Lyn Townsend/Andrea Sprenger
Willowbrook View, Downend, Horsley GL6 0PQ
Tel: 0845 458 9904
E-mail: inishfree@btinternet.com

IVAES

Anthroposophically-orientated and affiliated organisations, which are members of IVAES (international association of anthroposophical organisations for addiction therapy.

Germany

Akademie Wuppertal, Am Kriegermal 3a, D-42399 Wuppertal
Tel: 0049 202 612034 Fax: 0049 202 612218

Ergon, Beekloh 149, 22949 Ammersbek
Tel: 0049 40 6045915

Friedrich Daumer Haus, Am Schlossberg 1, D-36391 Schwarzenfels
Tel: 0049 6664 8340 Fax: 0049 6664 7596

Hiram Initiativen, Gotenstrasse 12, D-10829 Berlin Schoenberg
Tel: 0049 30 7883053 Fax: 0049 30 7883464

Lebens und Werkgemeinschaft Leimbach
Junker-Hoos-Strasse 4, D-34628 Willinghausen Leimbach
Tel: 0049 6691 5312 Fax: 0049 6691 6126

PAR-CE-VAL
Sakrower Landstrasse 68-70, D-14089 Berlin
Tel: 030 364 313 73 Fax: 030 364 313 75
E-mail: par.ce.val@gmx.de

Sieben Zwerge, Heilstätte
Grünwangener Strasse 4, D-88682 Salem Oberstenweiler
Tel: 0049 7544 5070 Fax: 0049 7544 50751

Syanon, Herzbergerstrasse 84, D-10365 Berlin Lichtenberg
Tel: 0049 30 55000 0 Fax: 0049 30 55000 220

Switzerland

Fondation La Clairière, CH-1832 Chamby
Tel: 0041 21 964 3453 Fax: 0041 21 964 3188

VEGA, Bahnhofstrasse 60, Postfach CH-4132 Muttenz 1
Tel: 0041 61 462 1362 Fax: 0041 61 462 1366

Other books from Hawthorn Press

FORTHCOMING
IN PAPERBACK

In Place of the Self
How drugs work
R Dunselman

Why are heroin, alcohol, hashish, ecstasy, LSD and tobacco attractive substances for so many people? Why are unusual visionary and 'high' experiences so important to users? These and other questions about drugs and drug use are answered comprehensively in this book.

304pp; 216 x 138mm; 1 903458 26 9; paperback.

Manhood
An action plan for changing men's lives
Steve Biddulph

'Most men don't have a life.' So begins the most powerful, practical and honest book ever to be written about men and boys. Not

about our problems – but about how we can find the joy and energy of being in a male body with a man's mind and spirit – about men's liberation.

Steve Biddulph, author of *Raising Boys* and the million-seller *The Secret of Happy Children,* writes about the turning point that men have reached. He gives practical personal answers to how things can be different from the bedroom to the workplace. He tells powerful stories about healing the rift between fathers and sons. About friendship. How women and men can get along in dynamic harmonious ways. How boys can be raised to be healthy men.

Manhood has had a profound emotional impact on tens of thousands of readers worldwide, and has been passed from son to father, friend to friend, husband to wife, with the simple message 'You must read this!'

272pp; 216 x 138mm; 1 869 890 99 X; paperback.

'Steve Biddulph should be in the UK what he is in Australia, the household name in the business of raising boys and being a man.'
Dorothy Rowe, psychologist and writer

Free Range Education
How home education works
Terri Dowty (ed)

FREE RANGE EDUCATION

How home education works

Edited by Terri Dowty

Welcome to this essential handbook for families considering or starting out in home education. *Free Range Education* is full of family stories, resources, burning questions, humour, tips, practical steps and useful advice so you can choose what best suits your family situation. You are already your child's main teacher and these families show how home education can work for you. Both parents and children offer useful guidance, based on their experience.

256pp; 210 x 148mm; cartoons; 1 903458 07 2; paperback.

Free to Learn

Introducing Steiner Waldorf Early Childhood Education

Lynne Oldfield

Free to Learn
Introducing Steiner Waldorf early childhood education
Lynne Oldfield

Free to Learn is a unique guide to the principles and methods of Steiner Waldorf early childhood education. This authoritative introduction is written by Lynne Oldfield, Director of the London Steiner Waldorf Early Childhood Teacher Training course. She draws on kindergarten experience from around the world, with stories, helpful insights, lively observations and pictures. This inspiring book will interest parents, educators and early years students. It is up to date, comprehensive, includes many photos and has a 16 page colour section.

256pp; 216 x 138mm; photographs; 1 903458 06 4; paperback.

Parenting Matters
Ways to bring up your children using heart and head
Parent Network

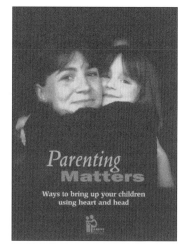

Parenting Matters helps you bring up loving and happy children. Here is the heart to becoming the more confident, sensitive relaxed, firm and caring parent that you truly are – enjoying your children and family.

Parenting Matters is a workbook packed with ideas, exercises and examples for personal use. It supports your learning on the course run by Parent Network. This sensible and positive approach has been successfully developed by parents for parents over many years.

Contents include:
    understanding children's needs and behaviour;
    positive communication; assertiveness;
    listening;
    dealing with feelings;
    building self-esteem;
    love and discipline;
    looking after parents' needs;
    setting up support groups.

228pp; 297 x 210mm; 1 869 890 16 7; paperback.

Being a Parent
Parent Network

Being a parent is one of the most important jobs in the world, because parents hold the future in their hands. Parents need all the help they can get. Yet many battle on without any support or guidance.

There are many different approaches to parenting. In our multi-cultural world, there is no one way of bringing up children that is right for everyone. *Being a Parent* helps you find out what works best for you and your children. This friendly and helpful book can be used on its own or as a workbook for the Parent Network course, Understanding Children 1, which is accredited by the National Open College Network.

96pp; 297 x 210mm; 1 869 890 81 7; paperback.

'Parent Network courses have brought smiles to the faces, and deep sighs of relief to thousands of parents all over the UK. A chance to sort out your thinking and raise your kids in the way you really want to, instead of in a series of knee-jerk reactions.'
                    Steve Biddulph, family therapist and parenting author

Parents' Comments:
'It is changing my life – wish I could have done this years ago.'
'This course has really helped improve our family life.'
'I have learnt some very good ideas to help me get on better with my children.'

Getting in touch with Hawthorn Press

What are your pressing questions about education?
The Hawthorn Education Series arises from parents' and educators' pressing questions and concerns – so please contact us with your questions. These will help spark new books and workshops if there is sufficient interest. We will be delighted to hear your views on our Education books, how they can be improved, and what your needs are.

Visit our website for details of the Education Series and forthcoming books and events:

http://www.hawthornpress.com

Ordering books

If you have difficulties ordering Hawthorn Press books from a bookshop, you can order direct from:

United Kingdom
Scottish Book Source Distribution,
137 Dundee Street, Edinburgh,
EH11 1BG
Tel: 0131 229 6800 Fax: 0131 229 9070

North America
Anthroposophic Press c/o Books International,
PO Box 960,
Herndon, VA 201 72-0960.
Toll free order line: 800-856-8664
Toll free fax line: 800-277-9747

Dear Reader

If you wish to follow up your reading of this book, please tick the boxes below as appropriate, fill in your name and address and return to Hawthorn Press:

☐ Please send me a catalogue of other Hawthorn Press books.

☐ Please send me details of Education series books.

Questions I have about Education are:

_____

_____

_____

_____

_____

Name _____

Address _____

_____

_____

Postcode _____ Tel. no. _____

Please return to: Hawthorn Press, Hawthorn House,
1 Lansdown Lane, Stroud, Glos. GL5 1BJ, UK
or Fax (01453) 751138

AMF